MAX notes®

F. Scott Fitzgerald

The Great Gatsby

Text by
Mary Dillard
(M.A., University of Texas at Dallas)
Department of English
Highland Park High School
Dallas, Texas

Illustrations by
Thomas E. Cantillon

P9-DMM-186

Research & Education Association
Visit our website at
www.rea.com

Research & Education Association
61 Ethel Road West
Piscataway, New Jersey 08854
E-mail: info@rea.com

MAXnotes® for
THE GREAT GATSBY

Published 2013

Copyright © 1994 by Research & Education Association, Inc. All rights reserved. No part of this book may be reproduced in any form without permission of the publisher.

Printed in the United States of America

Library of Congress Control Number 94-65952

ISBN-13: 978-0-87891-942-0
ISBN-10: 0-87891-942-2

MAXnotes® and REA® are registered trademarks of Research & Education Association, Inc.

What **MAXnotes** *Will Do for You*

This book is intended to help you absorb the essential contents and features of F. Scott Fitzgerald's *The Great Gatsby* and to help you gain a thorough understanding of the work. The book has been designed to do this more quickly and effectively than any other study guide.

For best results, this **MAXnotes** book should be used as a companion to the actual work, not instead of it. The interaction between the two will greatly benefit you.

To help you in your studies, this book presents the most up-to-date interpretations of every section of the actual work, followed by questions and fully explained answers that will enable you to analyze the material critically. The questions also will help you to test your understanding of the work and will prepare you for discussions and exams.

Meaningful illustrations are included to further enhance your understanding and enjoyment of the literary work. The illustrations are designed to place you into the mood and spirit of the work's settings.

The **MAXnotes** also include summaries, character lists, explanations of plot, and chapter-by-chapter analyses. A biography of the author and discussion of the work's historical context will help you put this literary piece into the proper perspective of what is taking place.

The use of this study guide will save you the hours of preparation time that would ordinarily be required to arrive at a complete grasp of this work of literature. You will be well prepared for classroom discussions, homework, and exams. The guidelines that are included for writing papers and reports on various topics will prepare you for any added work which may be assigned.

The **MAXnotes** will take your grades "to the max."

Larry B. Kling
Chief Editor

Contents

Each chapter includes List of Characters, Summary, Analysis, Study Questions and Answers, and Suggested Essay Topics.

SECTION ONE

Introduction

The Life and Work of F. Scott Fitzgerald

Francis Scott Key Fitzgerald, now regarded as the spokesman for the "Lost Generation" of the 1920s, was born in St. Paul, Minnesota, in 1896. His childhood and youth seem, in retrospect, as poetic as the works he later wrote. The life he lived became "the stuff of fiction," the characters and the plots a rather thinly-disguised autobiography. Like Jay Gatsby, the title character of his most famous novel, Fitzgerald created a vision which he wanted to become, a "Platonic conception of himself," and "to this conception he was faithful to the end."

Fitzgerald was educated at parochial prep schools where he received strict Roman Catholic training. The religious instruction never left him. Ironically, he was denied burial in a Catholic cemetery because of his rather uproarious lifestyle which ended in depression and alcoholism. In the fall of 1909, during his second year at St. Paul Academy, Fitzgerald began publishing in the school magazine. Sent East for a disciplined education, he entered The Newman School, whose student body came from wealthy Catholic families all over the country. At The Newman School he developed a friendship and intense rapport with Father Sigourney Webster Fay, a trustee and later headmaster of the school and the prototype for a character in *This Side of Paradise*, Fitzgerald's first novel, published in 1920.

Upon his grandmother's death, Fitzgerald and the family received a rather handsome inheritance, yet Scott seemed always to be cast into a society where others enjoyed more affluence than he. However, like Gatsby, a self-made man, Fitzgerald became the embodiment of the American Dream—an American Don Quixote.

Thanks to another relative's money, Fitzgerald was able to enroll in Princeton in 1913. He never graduated from the Ivy League school; in fact, he failed several courses during his undergraduate years. However, he wrote revues for the Triangle Club, Princeton's musical comedy group, and "donned swishy, satiny dresses to romp onstage" alongside attractive chorus girls. Years later, after enjoying some literary fame, he was asked to speak at Princeton, an occasion which endeared the school to him in new ways. Today, Princeton houses his memoirs, including letters from Ernest Hemingway, motion picture scripts, scrapbooks, and other mementos.

He withdrew from Princeton and entered the war in 1917, commissioned a second lieutenant in the army. While in Officers Candidate School in Alabama, he met and fell in love with Zelda Sayre, a relationship which is replicated in Jay Gatsby's obsession with Daisy and her fascination with a military man. He never made it to the European front, but he did come to the attention of New York publishers by the end of the war. Despite Zelda's breaking their engagement, they became re-engaged that fall. Their marriage produced one daughter—Scottie, who died in 1986. In 1919 his earnings totaled $879; the following year, following the publication of *This Side of Paradise*, an instant success, his earnings increased to $18,000.

By 1924 it was clear that Fitzgerald needed a change. He, Zelda, and Scottie moved to Europe, near the French Riviera, where he first met Ernest Hemingway, Gertrude Stein, and Edith Wharton. Before long, Zelda met and had an affair with Edouard Josanne, a relationship which Fitzgerald at first ignored but ultimately forced to a showdown. His writing may have profited because of her affair—according to biographer Andrew Turnbull, Fitzgerald's jealousy "sharpened the edge of Gatsby's and gave weight to Tom Buchanan's bullish determination to regain his wife."

To increase earnings he wrote some 160 short stories for

magazines, works which, by his own admission, lacked luster. After Zelda's alcoholism had several times forced her commitment to an institution, Scott went to Hollywood to write screenplays, and struggled unsuccessfully to complete a final novel, *The Last Tycoon*. He died in December of 1940 after a lifelong battle with alcohol and a series of heart attacks.

As early as 1920, Fitzgerald had in mind a tragic novel. He wrote to the president of Princeton that his novel would "say something fundamental about America, that fairy tale among nations." He saw our history as a great pageant and romance, the history of all aspiration—not just the American dream but the human dream—and, he wrote, "If I am at the end of it that too is a place in the line of the pioneers." Perhaps because of that vision, he has been called America's greatest modern romantic writer, a purveyor of timeless fiction with a gift of evocation that has yet to be surpassed. His works reflect the spirit of his times, yet they are timeless.

One cannot fail to notice how much of himself Fitzgerald put into all his work; he spoke of writing as a "sheer paring away of oneself." A melange of characters replicate or at least suggest people in his acquaintance. Gatsby seems almost to be an existential extension of Fitzgerald's posture, a persona created perhaps as a premonition of his own tragic end.

The almost poetic craftsmanship of Fitzgerald's prose, combined with his insight into the American experience, presented an imperishable portrait of his age, securing for him a permanent and enviable place in literary history.

Historical Background

The Great Gatsby, published in 1925, pictures the wasted American Dream as it depicts the 1920s in America. It speaks to every generation of readers, its contemporaneity depending in part on its picturesque presentation of that decade Fitzgerald himself labeled the "Jazz Age" and in part on its commentary concerning the human experience. The externals change—the attire, the songs, the fads—but its value and nostalgic tone transcend these externals. The novel provides the reader with a wider, panoramic vision of the American Dream, with a challenge to introspection if the reader reads sensitively and engages with the text.

The novel paints a vivid picture of America after World War I. From the postwar panic and realism evolved a shaking of social morés, a loss of innocence, a culture shock. Values of the old generation were rejected, with fashions including skirts above the knee and bobbed hair; a Bohemian lifestyle appeared with little moral or religious restraint; and innovative dances and musical forms that were considered by some to be obscene became the rage. It was a time of high living and opulence.

At the same time, the popular *carpe diem* ("seize the day") lifestyle and frivolity reflected an extreme feeling of alienation and nonidentity. A sense of melancholy and nostalgia existed, a discontent characterized by longing for conditions as they used to be. Americans were disenchanted. The war had promised so much; the results were disillusioning.

In addition, the availability of the automobile contributed to a carefree moral stance. No longer did young people have to court in the parlor, under parents' watchful eyes, for the car provided an escape from supervision. Historian Frederick Lewis Allen, in a study of "why the younger generation runs wild," refers to the automobile as a "house of prostitution on wheels." Prohibition, created by the Eighteenth Amendment, was violated widely, the results being the bootleggers, speakeasies, and underworld activities now commonly associated with the 1920s. These elements typify the decade Fitzgerald pictured in his novels.

As a result of this distance between expectations and reality, a chasm illustrated in the novel's scenario, a social satire develops. The etymology of *satire*, originally meaning "a dish of mixed fruit" or "potpourri," figures into the story as Fitzgerald fills the tapestry with every conceivable type in society. None of them seems happy. Acquiring a fortune by illicit means, Fitzgerald implies, will produce little happiness. A strong case can, therefore, be made that *The Great Gatsby* is social satire. The *zeitgeist*, the temper of the times, becomes extremely important: the milieu in which Fitzgerald lived and wrote shapes the content and the message of the book.

Fitzgerald's picture parallels that of *The Wasteland* by T. S. Eliot, a poet whose beliefs and poetry influenced Fitzgerald as he wrote *The Great Gatsby*. As a purveyor of the belief that we have wasted our dream, that we have turned our green continent into a veritable waste land, Fitzgerald was, perhaps, a prophet, a seer.

In one way, this novel is a Horatio Alger story with the conventional rags-to-riches motif; and, as such, it presents the unspoiled, untainted original American Dream. Jay Gatsby rises like Icarus above his rather shiftless parents to the riches of Midas, first witnessing a flamboyant lifestyle as cabin boy on the yacht of Dan Cody, a setting replete with alcohol, women, and ubiquitous parties. Such is the presentation of the American Dream. Ironically, the only ways to achieve such dreams are sordid and degraded.

The conclusion of his experience convinces Nick that we have made a mess of the "green breast of the New World," the world that the Dutch settlers saw when they came to this continent. A tawdry dream of self-love, greed, and corruption replaced the wholesomeness of the original dream founded on virtues and moral standards. A reliable picture of America in the 1920s, and at once a glamourized presentation of such meretricious living, *The Great Gatsby* has become a touchstone by which we measure quality of life in present-day America.

Although he was an artist, not a historian, he produced one of the most timeless and reliable pictures of this time in America's past, a veritable historical document. This "lost generation," to use Gertrude Stein's famous phrase, found a spokesman in Fitzgerald.

Master List of Characters

Nick Carraway—*the narrator. Thirty years old, he is a moralist who becomes a foil to every other character. He lives next door to Jay Gatsby and, thus, becomes Gatsby's link to Daisy, his cousin.*

Jay Gatsby—*the title character. A romantic idealist, he devotes his life to amassing wealth which he believes will win Daisy and thus fulfill his dream.*

Daisy Buchanan—*Nick's cousin, Tom's wife, and Gatsby's dream girl. Incapable of love, she represents the idolized upper class.*

Tom Buchanan—*Daisy's husband. Incapable of feeling guilt or any other emotion, he represents brutality, the moral carelessness of the rich, pseudo-intellectualism, and racism.*

Jordan Baker—*a friend of Daisy's from Louisville. A young and compulsively dishonest professional golfer, she is ironically involved with Nick, whose identifying characteristic is honesty. She, too, has no emotions and represents the coldness and cruelty of the rich.*

George Wilson—*proprietor of a garage in the Valley of Ashes. He represents the fate of the common working man, an "everyman" who believes a strong work ethic will eventually capture for him the American Dream.*

Myrtle Wilson—*George's wife. Her vitality attracts Tom. She wants to escape her lower class status, yet has no sense of values.*

Owl-Eyes—*a middle-aged "fair-weather" friend of Gatsby's.*

Pammy Buchanan—*daughter of Tom and Daisy. She appears as a possession to be displayed. Always dressed in white like her mother, she represents the shallowness of her parents.*

Henry C. Gatz—*Gatsby's father. He is proud of his son's prosperity.*

Meyer Wolfsheim—*a representative of the underworld. He has used Gatsby as a front man and is proud of his connections. Gatsby tells Nick that Wolfsheim is the man who fixed the 1919 World Series.*

Catherine—*Myrtle's sister. She is always available to have a good time.*

Mr. and Mrs. McKee—*tenants in a New York City hotel; they attend a party with the main characters.*

Ewing Klipspringer—*a "boarder" at Gatsby's house.*

Michaelis—*owner of a coffee shop near George Wilson's garage, who befriends George.*

Mr. Sloane—*a neighbor of Gatsby's who stops by while horseback riding.*

Summary of the Novel

The narrator of the story, Nick Carraway, has just returned from war and, restless in the West, goes East to work. In flashbacks he reveals the story of Jay Gatsby, his next-door neighbor, as he learns it. The nine chapters develop around seven parties interspersed with flashbacks.

Immediately after Nick moves to West Egg, he visits Daisy Buchanan, his second cousin "once-removed," and her husband Tom, a fellow Yale graduate, for dinner. Here Nick meets Jordan Baker, Daisy's friend from Louisville, who reveals that Tom is having an affair with Myrtle Wilson, the wife of a garage owner in the Valley of Ashes. Nick is shocked at the lack of morality in every level: the *nouveau riche*, the "old money," and those with no money at all.

Not long after, at the second party, Tom introduces Nick to Myrtle, who invites her sister Catherine and the McKees, residents in the hotel where the party takes place in New York City, to complete the guest list. At Gatsby's first party in West Egg, Nick meets a myriad of high-profile guests, most of whom have not been invited, all of whom ignore the statute concerning prohibition. The atmosphere is much like that of "an amusement park." The next party is lunch in town with Meyer Wolfsheim, one of Gatsby' business "connections," and obviously an underworld character.

Next, Tom and Daisy attend one of Gatsby's parties. By this time, Gatsby has used Nick, his next-door neighbor and Daisy's cousin, to set up a rendezvous with this young lady he had wanted to marry five years before. Daisy had married Tom Buchanan because of his immense wealth. Through the intervening years, Gatsby had managed to amass a fortune greater than Tom's and idealistically believes Daisy will leave Tom for him. Another party at Gatsby's mansion includes Tom and Daisy and a litany of diverse guests. The final catastrophic party at the Plaza Hotel in New York provides Tom the opportunity to confront Gatsby about his obsession with Daisy and Gatsby's alleged underworld activities.

Driving home from New York City, Daisy strikes and kills Myrtle Wilson with Gatsby's car. Gatsby, however, tells Nick that Daisy was driving the car. After tracing the yellow car to Gatsby, George Wilson shoots Gatsby to death in his pool and turns the gun on himself.

After Gatsby's poorly-attended funeral, Nick returns to the Midwest, disillusioned and disgusted by the experience.

Structure of the Novel

In the tradition of Geoffrey Chaucer's *The Canterbury Tales* and Joseph Conrad's *Heart of Darkness*, this novel is structured as a frame tale. From as early as the Middle Ages, writers of English have employed the device of framing a story with another story. The experience in *The Great Gatsby* is actually Nick Carraway's, not Jay Gatsby's. He relates Gatsby's story. Because Nick is a moral exemplar from start to finish, the reader sees him as a reliable narrator; we can believe his account of Gatsby.

By the second page of the novel, the story becomes an account of Gatsby's story as told in flashbacks through Nick's point of view. This flashback structure can make it difficult to place the events of the novel in their proper time sequence. For an explanation of the proper sequence of events, see the Appendix at the end of this book.

The dominant effect of this literary convention is veracity: the reader can believe that what Nick says is truth. The end of the story appears in the beginning, for immediately the reader becomes aware that Nick is disenchanted with the immorality of the East and wants to return to the West. After his "privileged glimpse into the heart," a journey he does not wish to repeat, the story turns to Nick's perceptions of Gatsby and of Long Island. Gatsby's dream almost replicates that of the "Dutch sailors," who, in their discovery of the New World, found a latter-day Camelot. Such a similarity justifies Nick's belief that Gatsby's dream made him "worth more than the whole damn bunch put together." He had "an extraordinary gift for hope, a romantic readiness," that *almost* justified his illegal doings in the eyes of Nick.

Built upon the conventional rags-to-riches motif, this novel fits the mold of a Horatio Alger story. Typically, the poor boy risks himself to save the "damsel in distress" in a wagon pulled at breakneck speed by a runaway horse. As a result of saving the young lady, he works for her father, usually a man of means, and ultimately inherits her father's business and marries her. In a sense he raises himself by his "own bootstraps." Such is the ideal American Dream—an innocent, pure form of Thomas Jefferson's "pursuit of happiness." In Fitzgerald's parallel, "the poor boy," Gatsby, naïvely determines to amass wealth in whatever ways necessary, the implication being that nothing can preclude or obstruct his winning the damsel's hand. Like the archetypal Cinderella story, the most deserving must always win Prince Charming and become heir to a massive fortune. Tragically, Gatsby had learned well from American society that dishonesty and illicit means of procuring a fortune will win what pure love and resolve cannot.

Estimated Reading Time

An average reader can complete the novel in four to five hours. A close reading will take longer perhaps, but even reading critically, the reading should not require much more than five hours.

The Great Gatsby

Chapter 1

New Characters:

Nick Carraway: *the narrator of the story*

Daisy Buchanan: *Nick's cousin*

Tom Buchanan: *Daisy's husband and a fellow Yale graduate of Nick's*

Jordan Baker: *a friend of Daisy and, eventually, a friend of Nick Carraway*

Jay Gatsby: *Nick's mysterious next-door neighbor*

Summary

Soon after Nick Carraway returns from the war, he abandons his native Middle West and the hardware business of his forebears and goes East to enter the bond business. He rents a bungalow in West Egg, Long Island, the "less fashionable" of two peninsulas, and finds his house sandwiched between two huge houses that rent "for twelve or fifteen thousand a season."

Across the bay, in East Egg, live Nick's cousin Daisy and her husband Tom, who invite Nick for tea. Jordan Baker, a female golfer and friend of Daisy, informs Nick of Tom's affair with Myrtle Wilson in a noticeably nonchalant manner. Nick's reaction is that Daisy should "rush out of the house" and escape this immoral situation. She does not. Tom engages Nick in conversation, asking if he has read "The Rise of the Colored Empires" by Goddard. Tom concurs

with the author's thesis that the white race is in danger of being overwhelmed by Blacks. This theory, he argues, is all scientific.

After the get-together, Nick returns home and sees Jay Gatsby, his next-door neighbor, trembling, glancing seaward, looking at a single green light "that might have been the end of a dock." Just as quickly, Gatsby disappears from sight.

Analysis

In the frame of the novel Nick quotes his father as having said, "Whenever you feel like criticizing anyone, just remember that all the people in this world haven't had the advantages that you've had." At first the reader might think the advantages he alludes to are monetary, but then Nick acknowledges that he agrees with his father: "a sense of the fundamental decencies is parcelled out unequally at birth." Clearly, decency, not wealth, is the supreme value.

Nick immediately captures the confidence of the reader. Often "privy to the secret griefs of wild, unknown men," involuntarily making "riotous excursions with privileged glimpses into the human heart." Nick is trustworthy, a seer, even though he contends, "Most of the confidences were unsought." His are the traditional values from America's past. He acknowledges at the outset that Gatsby "represented everything" for which he had "an unaffected scorn"; paradoxically, however, he finds in Gatsby "something gorgeous," a dream quality with "some heightened sensitivity to the promises of life." It was not Gatsby that, ultimately, Nick rejected in New York; it was "what preyed on Gatsby, what foul dust floated in the wake of his dreams" that brought closure and finality to Nick's

rite of passage. Thus, the brief introduction to Nick, a reliable narrator, takes on singular importance in understanding Fitzgerald's message.

Even in these early stages of the novel, the writer prepares subtly for his ultimate message. Fitzgerald alludes to "Midas and Morgan and Mæcenas," men of vast fortunes from mythology and Greek civilizations and the recent past, as Nick buys "a dozen volumes on banking and credit and investment securities." These books stand on his shelf "in red and gold like new money from the mint, promising to unfold the shining secrets" of these barons of big finance. Juxtaposed to these names are references to this country's founders. When a newcomer to West Egg asks directions, Nick becomes a "guide, a pathfinder, an original settler." By juxtaposing these moneyed tycoons to the original "pathfinders" and "settlers," Fitzgerald subtly sets up the conflict between the untainted American Dream and the subsequent obsession with money. That Nick is enamored of such books suggests that even he can be impressed with wealth. That Tom explores books on racial prejudice as a science suggests that he is shallow, supercilious, and extremely snobby. This study of reading habits communicates significantly to the understanding of the characters.

At this early stage in the novel a reference to the Middle West as "the ragged edge of the universe," a rugged pioneer image, contrasts with the sophistication of the East, specifically New York City. The original settlers, those who came to the West, represent the quintessential work ethic while the moneyed people, or at least their descendants, represent a consumption ethic. Even dinner and after-dinner activities emphasize for Nick the difference in values. In the West an evening "was hurried from phase to phase toward its close," representative of the work ethic in contrast to the pleasure and relative unimportance of work in the East, where making the most money with the least amount of effort seems to be the goal. A person with such aspirations would be, in the words of Tom, "a God damned fool to live anywhere else." West Egg, in its eclectic "melting pot" neighborhood, takes on the symbolism and character of the Old West, the land discovered in the fulfillment of dreams. Conversely, elite East Egg comes across as sophisticated, superficial, and smug. To go anywhere, however, going from either East

Egg or West Egg, the road must pass through the Valley of Ashes, the waste perhaps representing the hollowness of the American Dream.

In the opening chapter, also, are references to color, images which proliferate throughout the novel. In addition to the red and gold books, white–here describing "palaces of fashionable East Egg," Daisy and Jordan's dresses, and, most ironically, their "beautiful white girlhood"—deepens in symbolic interpretation. Inverting the universal symbol, in this work white represents *im*purity, or loss of innocence. The Buchanans' mansion, "cheerful red-and-white," glows in the afternoon sun reflecting gold. Because of the disregard for traditional marriage vows, the whiteness is ironic. Pastels, in this instance "rosy-colored space," represent a fairy-tale, ephemeral quality, such as the unreality of the Buchanans' lifestyle. With little if any work to do, games become increasingly important. Daisy fatuously describes Nick as "a rose, an absolute rose." Later, Gatsby finds that a rose is a "grotesque thing" in an unreal world where ghosts, "breathing dreams like air," drift "for-

tuitously about."

Almost immediately, gray images are associated with decadence, decay, desolation, and waste—wasted vitality, wasted morals, and wasted dreams. Jordan Baker has "gray sun-strained eyes" looking out of a "wan" or pale, "discontented face"; she has "autumn-leaf yellow" hair, autumn being the archetypal symbol of death or dying. Although Nick is attracted to her, ultimately her lack of character closes out his interest. Being so often described with "gray" and autumn images connects her with decadence.

Finally, at the end of the chapter, Gatsby appears under the "silver pepper of the stars," looking longingly at "a single green light." Appearing almost like a glittering god, Gatsby often wears silver and gold. At one point, he wears a white flannel suit, silver shirt, and gold-colored tie. Seemingly, the point of the metaphors and descriptions of his attire is to reinforce the idea that he is a son of a god.

The green, introduced first as the light at the end of a dock, has ambivalent interpretations. Green typically is associated with growth, spring, and new life. It signals "Go! Go! Go!" presumably for any generation. It is the color of money. All of these meanings apply in *The Great Gatsby*. Primarily, it is connected with Daisy, who turns out to be an unworthy dream. Colors, then, not only vivify images and create a picturesque vista for the reader but also facilitate Fitzgerald's thematic commentary about reality and dreams.

Juxtaposed with Nick's conclusion that "life is much more successfully looked at from a single window after all" is the contrast of two "windows" or discrete worlds—East Egg and West Egg. A bird's eye view shows identically-contoured formations of land, "enormous eggs," separated only by "a courtesy bay." To the wingless counterpart, however, the eggs are dissimilar in "every particular except shape and size." On West Egg, "the less fashionable of the two," appear houses designed and built with no apparent restrictions or codes, a bungalow sandwiched between two mansions. By contrast, the houses on fashionable East Egg "glittered" with "white palaces." The contrasting descriptions focus on *nouveau riche* or new money, with the possible implication of lack of refinement or class, and old money, with well-groomed houses and lawns accompanying well-groomed, well-bred occupants, who, at least superficially, are characterized by gentility.

The pursuit of this distorted American Dream leads to worship at unworthy shrines: beauty, youth, and pleasure become icons, gods unworthy of worship yet traceable as a quest as far back as Ponce de Leon, who searched for the Fountain of Youth. Resulting from the pursuit of these "ideals" are restlessness and unfulfilled lives. To reinforce this flawed concept and its effects, images of "restlessness" and "drifting" recur numerous times in the novel. Tom, forever living in the afterglow of his New Haven football days, now brings down a "string of polo ponies" from Lake Forest, seemingly to extend into adulthood collegiate activities; he "would drift on forever seeking, a little wistfully, for the dramatic turbulence of some irrecoverable football game." Standing in riding clothes with legs apart, he appears aggressive, supercilious, "with a touch of paternal contempt," a trait which Daisy emphasizes, to Tom's chagrin. At one of Gatsby's parties, Tom is introduced as the polo player, another description he detests. Later in this chapter, when Daisy mentions Pammy, their daughter, Tom hovers "restlessly about the room."

Descriptive "tags" or epithets, another use of recurring words to describe the principal characters, enable the reader to visualize the characters. Tom is restless, careless, physical. He has drifted, "unrestfully," and he will drift on forever, a defiant willfulness seeking fulfillment. His eyes flash restlessly. He hovers restlessly. He has "a supercilious manner, arrogant eyes." He always leans "aggressively forward," with enormous physical power, evidenced by a "great pack of muscle." He has a cruel body "capable of enormous leverage," but his voice is a "gruff, husky tenor" with a touch of "paternal contempt" in it. Jordan's chin is lifted a little; she seems to be balancing some object on it, her body thrown backward at the shoulders "like a young cadet." She has a "wan, charming discontented face," and later she is described as having a "bored haughty face." The tag which recurs in her description is *jauntiness*. At a party, Nick observes that she wears evening dresses, all her dresses, like sports clothes—"there was a jauntiness about her movements as if she had first learned to walk upon golf courses on clean, crisp mornings." As she leaves Nick, her brown hand waves "a jaunty salute." Both she and Daisy are described like the curtains: their white dresses are "rippling and fluttering." Daisy's low, thrilling voice, perhaps a charming power play to cause people to "lean toward her," resurfaces often enough in the story to undoubtedly serve a literary purpose. "The exhilarating ripple of her voice was a wild tonic in the rain" to Gatsby when they were reunited. Even in girlhood, "something in that voice of hers" had compelled those around her. Similar references in subsequent chapters reinforce these descriptions.

The images which portray setting are no less picturesque and permanent than those which characterize. Compare, for example, the descriptions of the two houses: Gatsby's estate and the Buchanans' "cheerful red-and-white Georgian Colonial mansion." Gatsby's "enormous house," which makes Nick's bungalow look like "an eyesore," is a "factual imitation of some Hotel de Ville in Normandy, with a tower on one side covered by a "thin beard of raw ivy." It is located on 40 acres of lawn and garden; it has "halls and salons and verandas" and a "high Gothic library, panelled with carved English oak," probably transported complete from some ruin overseas. It is a "feudal silhouette against the sky," a kind of period piece, hearkening back to the past. By contrast, Tom and Daisy's place gleams with brightness, the lawn starting at the beach and running toward the front door "for a quarter of a mile, jumping over sun-dials and brick walks and burning gardens." Through such metaphors as "thin *beard* of raw ivy" and personification of the lawn leaping over sundials, Fitzgerald creates poetic, picturesque images which vivify and make permanent the prose of the novel.

Finally, the image that closes the chapter, Gatsby, trembling, standing with outstretched arms, looking at the blinking green light at the end of a dock, takes on greater significance as the work progresses. Nick understands only that this silhouette is his neighbor and that a certain mystique or mystery surrounds him. This image reinforces the dreamlike quality of this hero on a quest to attain his dream. And it is this "heightened sensitivity to the promises of life" that causes Nick to see in Gatsby an "extraordinary gift for hope, a romantic readiness" that he has never seen before nor is he likely to see again. Ironically, this final scene in Chapter 1 provides transition and contrast to the first paragraphs of Chapter 2—well-manicured lawns and the pristine water of the bay are jarringly juxtaposed with the squalor and foul river running through the Valley of Ashes, a most significant and deft contrast between dream and reality.

Study Questions

1. Who is the narrator of the story?
2. What is the significance of the white space between paragraphs 4 and 5?
3. From what part of the country does Nick originally come?
4. Why has Nick moved to New York?
5. How does Nick come to live next door to Jay Gatsby?
6. Where had Nick known Tom Buchanan before?
7. What is Jordan Baker's relationship to Daisy Buchanan?
8. What does Nick learn from Jordan when Tom is called to the phone?

9. What is the "secret society"?

10. What does Nick see Gatsby doing at the end of the chapter?

Answers

1. Nick Carraway tells the story as he learns it from various sources.

2. The white space indicates where the flashback to Nick's experience in New York begins.

3. The Midwest is the home of Nick and his ancestors, a part of the country in touch with the soil and wholesome American values.

4. After the war, he is looking for a better job than the Midwest provides.

5. He rents a bungalow with a friend who subsequently transfers to Washington, leaving Nick without a roommate.

6. They had been in school together at Yale.

7. The two had been friends in Louisville, Kentucky. Daisy is two years older than Jordan.

8. Tom has "a woman" in New York. Jordan enjoys eavesdropping.

9. The "secret society" consists of distinguished people who, seemingly, are above the law; their social standing is power.

10. Gatsby is stretching out his arms toward a green light at the end of a dock across the water in a worshipful stance.

Suggested Essay Topics

1. Consider the references to people in literature or history in the chapter. What purpose(s) do they serve?

2. Write a character sketch of Daisy (or Tom or Jordan), focusing on the recurring "tag" used to describe them. Daisy leans forward and talks in a low voice; Tom is restless and hulking; Jordan balances something on her chin almost in an athletic stance. What is Fitzgerald's purpose in thus describing them?

3. Explain how the first chapter of this novel is critically important in the development of plot, characters, and themes.

Chapter 2

New Characters:

George Wilson: *Myrtle's husband; owner of an automobile repair shop where cars are also bought and sold*

Myrtle Wilson: *George's wife and Tom's mistress; in her middle 30s and "faintly stout"*

Catherine: *Myrtle's sister, "a slender, worldly girl of about thirty, with a solid sticky bob of red hair" who functions as Nick's companion at Myrtle's request*

Mr. & Mrs. McKee: *a couple who live in the hotel where Tom, Myrtle, and Nick go for a party*

Summary

Tom invites Nick to go to the city with him. They pass through the Valley of Ashes, "a fantastic farm where ashes grow like wheat into ridges and hills and grotesque gardens." The area which holds the ashes of cars and trains is bounded by a "small foul river." Hovering over the Valley of Ashes is the long-forgotten billboard of an oculist, Dr. T. J. Eckleburg, the eyes "dimmed a little by many paintless days under sun and rain," brooding "over the solemn dumping ground." Enormous spectacles "pass over a non-existent nose."

Tom and Nick arrive at the auto garage of George Wilson. Wilson and Tom exchange comments about a car Tom may sell. Tom arranges for Wilson's wife Myrtle to take the next train to New York for a romantic tryst.

In town Myrtle purchases a gossip magazine, some beauty aids, and a dog. She changes clothes at the apartment, putting on a dress Tom has provided, and reappears in "panting vitality." When Myrtle's sister Catherine asks Nick about Gatsby, having ascertained that Nick lives on West Egg, she repeats some of the rumors that are circulating about him. Additionally, she brings up the explanation of her sister's relationship with Tom; of Daisy, she explains, "She's a Catholic, and they don't believe in divorce." Nick knows Daisy is not Catholic. Myrtle explains her disdain for George, who is not "fit to lick" her shoe. The fine clothes of Tom had at first attracted her—she could not keep her eyes off him. However, when Myrtle speaks of Daisy to Tom, he reprimands her, saying she has no right to "mention Daisy's name." When she persists, Tom unemotionally strikes her, one deft blow breaking her nose.

Nick admits to having been drunk just twice in his life, the

second time being that afternoon. Like all the other guests, he too is drunk. What he reads is distorted—it makes no sense to him. An observer of the action, and to some extent a participant, Nick decides he is both "within and without" that hotel room, "simultaneously enchanted and repelled by the inexhaustible variety of life." He finds himself in Pennsylvania Station, waiting for the four o'clock train.

Analysis

The Valley of Ashes, like T. S. Eliot's poem *The Wasteland*, published in 1922, conveys the concept of America's wasted opportunities. This contrast of settings is tantamount to understanding Fitzgerald's theme, a poetic criticism concerning America's opportunities and the mess we have made of our golden age, a message Fitzgerald communicates in a subtle but effective manner.

Placing the description of the Valley of Ashes immediately after the description of the green light at the end of Chapter 1 provides a stark contrast. That juxtaposition of the color images—green with gray—highlights the theme of waste. The green of life and growth has been turned to waste through industrialization. Motorcars and trains, great advancements in industrialization have, nevertheless, left debris behind. As it turns out, the light at the end of Daisy's dock represents wasted moral fiber, too. She is not a paragon of virtue. Like others of the idle rich on East Egg, Fitzgerald implies, she is tainted by self-love, by opulence, and by a hedonistic lifestyle.

Interestingly, the valley is described in farming or agrarian terms: "a fantastic *farm* where ashes *grow like wheat* into ridges and hills and *grotesque gardens*," and "ash-gray men" appear with "*leaden spades*." Irony derives from the association of waste with the green light and of growth with the gray Valley of Ashes.

Camouflaging the Valley of Ashes, gray in all the descriptive phrases, is a "low whitewashed railroad fence," and "the only building in sight was a small block of yellow brick sitting on the edge of the waste land." This very direct reference to Eliot's *The Wasteland* underscores Fitzgerald's theme—we have wasted our vitality in pursuit of a materialism that does not satisfy. George Wilson, a pale spiritless man veiled with "white ashen dust," wiping

his hands on a "piece of waste," embodies that effete pursuit and, perhaps, represents Everyman. He may not have pulled himself up by the bootstraps, but he maintains a gleam of hope in "his light blue eyes."

Immediately introduced is the symbolic billboard of the eyes of Doctor T. J. Eckleburg, "looking out of no face" over a "nonexistent nose." Through the description emphasizing his "eternal blindness," the narrator seems to describe some kind of god looking with a vacant stare as he describes the oculist who forgot his practice and moved away. That the eyes *brood* over the "solemn dumping ground" gives credibility to that symbolism. The God who allowed men to discover the New World has now ostensibly turned His back, His absence as unnoticed as Dr. T. J. Eckleburg's.

Ironically, Nick expects to see "a great flock of white sheep"— another farm or pastoral image—turn the corner near the hotel, and he describes the West Hundreds as "one slice in a long white cake of apartment houses," a description similar to the "frosted wedding-cake" ceiling in the description of the Buchanans' home in Chapter 1. However, after witnessing the goings-on of the afternoon he philosophically decides that the "line of yellow windows must have contributed their share of human secrecy to the casual watcher in the darkening streets": he was "within and without, simultaneously enchanted and repelled by the inexhaustible variety of life." So white continues to be inverted or insubstantial, unreal; the yellow or gold associated with money, at least marginally perverse; the gray, desolate and decadent. The pastels, too, seem

insubstantial and dreamlike. Things are not always what they appear to be.

Clothes and personal appearance are all-important in this presentation of the American Dream. Myrtle is transformed when she dons the outfits Tom provides for her; "hauteur" replaces or enhances her vitality. Ironically, when Mrs. McKee compliments the dress, she remarks, "It's just a crazy old thing" which she slips on when she does not care what she looks like. Additionally, it was Tom's clothes which first attracted her to him. He "had on a dress suit and patent leather shoes," and she admits she could not keep her eyes off him, his white shirt-front pressing against her arm. Conversely, George had to borrow the suit they were married in. Myrtle concludes he is not "fit to lick" her shoe and is so dumb "he doesn't know he's alive." Such "embarrassment" caused her to cry when the owner came to reclaim his suit.

Books and printed material are symbolic, just as clothes are. The books in Gatsby's library, acknowledged as real by a surprised Owl-Eyes, nevertheless have uncut pages, suggesting pseudo-intellectualism—doing things and owning things to suggest a respectability that may not exist. Tom reads and refers to books that echo his snobbish feeling of superiority or elitism, his prejudiced attitudes. Having been "rather literary in college," Nick "had the high intention" of reading many books. Myrtle's interests run to "some of the small scandal magazines of Broadway," such as *Town Tattle*, several copies of which lie on the table in the hotel room.

The convention of "withheld information" increases the interest both of the reader and of the narrator. Like Nick, we learn of Gatsby's past piecemeal, first hearing rumors which probably have no basis in fact. Catherine repeats the rumor she heard that "he's a nephew or a cousin of Kaiser Wilhelm's," and "that's where his money comes from." In addition to increasing suspense, the effect of this convention is to make Gatsby a type of god or demigod. In archetypal stories, the hero has a mysterious origin, often coming from the water, and a mysterious past. In between birth and death is an enigmatic, almost supernatural, life. Gatsby fulfills this myth in several different ways. He evolves and takes shape gradually, initially through unverifiable stories. As Nick pieces together such stories, he gains insight into Gatsby's background. The reader, too, gradually learns about this self-made man. Clearly, Gatsby's background is largely unknown, fodder for speculation. Nick, and the reader through Nick, continues to experience ambivalence toward Gatsby. Ironically, he epitomizes the American Dream, but he is an unworthy symbol.

Study Questions

1. What is the Valley of Ashes literally?

2. Who or what is Dr. T. J. Eckleburg?

3. What is George Wilson's occupation?

4. What items does Myrtle purchase in the city?

5. What is significant about Myrtle's questioning whether the dog is a boy or girl?

6. Who is Catherine?

7. What effect does the change of dress have on Myrtle?

8. How does Myrtle talk about the help at the hotel?

9. What rumor has Catherine heard about Gatsby?

10. How does Catherine explain to Nick the affair of Myrtle and Tom?

Answers

1. It is an area, something like an isthmus, joining West Egg and East Egg. It parallels a railroad track.

2. The picture of Dr. Eckleburg, an oculist in a bygone age, appears on a billboard in the Valley of Ashes.

3. Wilson pumps gas and repairs cars.

4. She purchases *Town Tattle* magazine, cold cream, perfume, and a puppy. She has another list to buy the next day: "a massage and a wave, and a collar for the dog, and one of those cute little ash-trays where you touch a spring, and a wreath with a black silk bow for mother's grave that'll last all summer."

5. She cannot acknowledge the sex of the dog—it is too deli-
    cate an issue—but she herself is involved in an illicit sexual
    relationship.

6. Catherine is Myrtle's sister procured as a companion for
    Nick. She may be a prostitute since she "lived with a girl
    friend at a hotel."

7. She is transformed as vitality changes to "impressive hau-
    teur."

8. She refers to them as an inferior order; she has changed roles
    as she has changed clothes.

9. He is a nephew or cousin of Kaiser Wilhelm's.

10. According to Catherine, Daisy is Catholic and refuses to give
    Tom a divorce.

Suggested Essay Topics

1. Consider the possibilities of an agrarian society being the
    epitome of the American Dream. Find evidences of farm-
    ing or pastoral scenes and diction in the first two chapters
    which suggest the belief that such a society fulfills the ideal
    American Dream.

2. Contrast the green light at the end of Chapter 1 and the gray
    images in the Valley of Ashes in Chapter 2. What thematic
    statement do the contrasting images reveal?

3. How can George Wilson be said to symbolize the American
    Dream? Consider the Horatio Alger ("rags-to-riches") motif,
    as well as his undying desire to better his situation.

4. Write about Fitzgerald's poetic style, focusing especially
    on the vivid metaphors and images, such as this descrip-
    tion from Catherine: "Her eyebrows had been plucked and
    then drawn on again at a more rakish angle, but the efforts
    of nature toward the restoration of the old alignment gave
    a blurred air to her face." How is Fitzgerald a disciplined
    writer with great control of his prose?

5. Research descriptions of archetypal heroes, including their mysterious beginnings associated with rumors and mythical power. Consider Gatsby as such a hero, based upon the rumors surrounding him.

Chapter 3

New Characters:

Gatsby's chauffeur: *in a uniform of "robin's-egg blue" he invites Nick to one of Gatsby's parties*

A pair of stage twins: *two young women, unnamed, in yellow dresses*

Owl-Eyes: *a "stout, middle-aged man, with enormous owl-eyed spectacles" who has been drunk for a week, sitting in Gatsby's library examining the books*

Summary

In Chapter 3 Gatsby's parties in general, and one in particular, are described in poetic fashion. Motorboats, aquaplanes, cars—these sources of amusement appear in great numbers. Food, in vast quantities and garishly prepared, comes in every Friday; once every two weeks a "corps of caterers" transforms Gatsby's grounds into an amusement park setting.

The guests conduct themselves "according to the rules of behavior associated with amusement parks." Liquor flows freely, uninvited guests stay virtually all night, and fights are rampant. The host himself never participates: "no one swooned backward on Gatsby, and no French bob touched Gatsby's shoulder, and no singing quartets were formed with Gatsby's head for one link." Rumors therefore emerge about him. Not knowing the facts, perhaps, the guests speculate on his business, his war experience, and his past. One visitor who at a previous party had torn a gown on a chair received from Gatsby a replacement dress—"gas blue with lavender beads." Interestingly, she knows the price—$265, information no doubt conveyed by the price tag's being left on it.

On this particular Saturday night, Nick, one of the few guests actually to receive an invitation to Gatsby's house, spends time with

Jordan Baker. In Gatsby's library he and Jordan encounter Owl-Eyes, a guest who claims to have been drunk for about a week. He has discovered that Gatsby's books are real, not *faux* cardboard. He reveals, however, that the pages have not been cut, obviously making the books impossible to read.

Finally, Nick meets someone who recognizes him from having been in the same battalion in World War I in Europe. Moments later he discovers that this man is Gatsby. Immediately, Nick is enamored of the man's smile and romantic qualities. When Jordan breaks in, Gatsby invites her into the house where he talks privately with her at least an hour. She asks Nick to call her later at the home of her aunt, Mrs. Sigourney Howard. Telling the guests

good-bye, Gatsby invites Nick to try out his new hydroplane the next morning. However, upon leaving, Nick observes a group of people gathered around a car which has been driven into a ditch. The wheel is completely off, but the inebriated occupants of the car—Owl-Eyes and another unnamed guest—want simply to call a service station for gasoline to get them on their way again.

Nick continues to study and work at his job, lunching with other accountants and dining in the evening at the Yale Club. He has a brief affair, terminated when the young lady's brother becomes somewhat hostile. In midsummer he begins to see Jordan again, at first flattered to be in the presence of this young lady golfer, then tenderly curious about her dishonesty. The story Nick had earlier tried and failed to remember now comes back to him; it concerned dishonesty in a golf tournament. Ironically, he chooses to overlook the incident, saying, "dishonesty in a woman is a thing you never blame deeply," but simultaneously he very objectively assesses himself as "one of the few honest people" he has ever known. Again the moral exemplar, he acknowledges matter-of-factly that he is "full of interior rules that act as brakes" on his desires. At that moment, he determines that the honest thing for him to do is to terminate a relationship with some young lady back home, the one everyone had expected him to marry. That had to be "tactfully broken off" before he was free.

Analysis

In this chapter the narrative and literary techniques continue to function in the same ways. Color images multiply. Cars and eyes as symbols recur. Rumors contributing to the image of archetypal heroes continue. The narrative voice and tags of description re-surface, enhancing and validating earlier assumptions.

Yellow predominates in the lush party setting at Gatsby's house. Gatsby's station wagon scampers "like a brisk yellow bug to meet all trains" bearing guests. Glittering food offerings include "turkeys bewitched to a dark gold." The orchestra plays "yellow cocktail music," the novelist employing synaesthesia (using one sense to describe another, here a color or sight image to describe a sound or auditory image) as part of the depiction of the age. The setting is "gaudy with primary colors" and with enough "colored lights to make a Christmas tree of Gatsby's enormous garden." Two girls at Nick's table wear "twin yellow dresses," and Jordan rests her "slender golden arm" on Nick's.

The color is thus subtly associated with luxury, opulence, and hedonism—the essence of the 1920s. Paradoxically, yellow is also the color of decay, of decadence. Coalescing with yellow images are pastels: Gatsby's chauffeur comes "in a uniform of robin's-egg blue" to invite Nick to the party, and the replacement evening gown is "gas blue with lavender beads." The "little villages in France" are "gray" in Gatsby's memory. The accented colors and their images convey themes no less effectively than symbols.

Probably the dominant symbol, perhaps equally important as the green light, is the automobile, the most symptomatic of the age. In addition to Gatsby's yellow station wagon, his Rolls Royce becomes an "omnibus," bearing guests to and from the city. Cars at the party are "parked five deep in the drive." The one in which Owl-Eyes was a passenger is a "new coupé" with the wheel detached. The very drunk guest insists he was not driving, that he knows next to nothing about driving. This accident seems to foreshadow the later one when Daisy is driving the "death car" which kills Myrtle. Another automobile accident involved Tom and a chambermaid at the Santa Barbara hotel where he and Daisy were staying three months after they were married. He "ran into a wagon on the Ventura road" and "ripped a front wheel off his car." Additionally, Jordan leaves a borrowed car out in the rain with the top down. Thus, the driving society, the recklessness with people's lives and morals, parallels the theme concerning wasted potential and wasted goodness.

The drunken Owl-Eyes also seems to repeat the message of the eyes of Dr. T. J. Eckleburg. The emphasis on eyes, later equated by George with the eyes of God, unites with the message hinted at through automobiles. Part of the picture—both of the 1920s and of Nick's exposure to high society—is the consumption of liquor. At this particular party, "the bar is in full swing, and floating rounds of cocktails permeate the garden." Champagne is "served in glasses bigger than finger bowls." Still, although the bar is crowded, "Gatsby was not there." The fact that he does not drink sets him apart from guests like Owl-Eyes who boasts of having been drunk "for about a week now." Prohibition, the law of the land, is ignored. Yet, rumors, undoubtedly to some extent based on fact, picture Gatsby as a bootlegger. To provide the liquor is as immoral as drinking it during prohibition.

This picture of the Jazz Age in Chapter 3 includes references to women's hair dyed and "shorn in strange new ways," to new dances, and to music—"by seven o'clock the orchestra has arrived, no thin five-piece affair, but a whole pitful of oboes and trombones and saxophones and viols and cornets and piccolos, and low and high drums." As the evening wanes, the moon rises higher, and "floating in the Sound was a triangle of silver scales, trembling a little to the stiff, tinny drip of the banjoes on the lawn." Old men danced with "flappers," pushing young girls "backward in eternal graceless circles, superior couples holding each other tortuously, fashionably and keeping in the corners." Finally, "the *Jazz History of the World*," Vladimir Tostoff's composition, is over. Replacing the music is "the caterwauling horns" of the cars leaving the party. As the horns "reached a crescendo," Nick observes Gatsby raising his hand in "a formal gesture of farewell." *Caterwauling*, or making the shrill sound of a cat's cry, recurs repeatedly in the description of horns—both automobile horns and saxophones—creating a lasting auditory image. This wail becomes synonymous with the Jazz Age. Such a vivid portrayal defines the "objective correlative," T. S. Eliot's term to describe "a set of objects, a situation, a chain of events which shall be the formula of that *particular* emotion." Therefore, when the "external facts" terminate in "sensory experience," an emotion is immediately evoked. Hence, when the caterwauling sound recurs, the reader is transported mentally and vicariously to the Jazz Age, during which such sounds were common.

Rumors continue to swirl about Gatsby. One of the girls in yellow shares the story she has heard: "Somebody told me they thought he killed a man once." Another argues, "It's more that he was a German spy during the war," and so those who "found little that it was necessary to whisper about in this world" speculate about the whispers concerning Gatsby. Nick can accept more readily that Gatsby "sprang from the swamps of Louisiana or from the lower East Side of New York" than that he drifted "coolly out of nowhere" and bought a palace on Long Island Sound. Ironically, he is closer to the truth than anyone else.

The narrative voice of Nick enables the reader to flesh out and interpret the tags used to describe the characters. Gatsby's repeated use of "Old Sport" and his rare smile, Jordan's "jauntiness" and her seeming to balance something on her chin, Nick's total candor in suspecting himself of possessing "at least one of the cardinal virtues," his being honest—these tags serve the purposes of characterizing, of lending validity to descriptions, and of continuing to develop theme. Finally, the picture of the partygoers presents a tawdry picture of America at play.

Irony more noticeably appears in the party scene. Early in the chapter the description of the party, buffet tables "garnished with glistening hors-d'oeuvre, spiced baked hams crowded against salads of harlequin designs and pastry pigs," evokes Petronius' *Satyricon* from the early classical literature of Rome. Trimalchio, the ostentatious hero of this ancient satire, also *nouveau riche*, provides such a colossal banquet. Eventually, Fitzgerald writes of Gatsby, his career "as Trimalchio was over." Such an allusion lends credibility to the belief that Fitzgerald did intend the novel as a type of satire; indeed, in a letter to his publisher in November of 1924 , he wrote that he had decided to name his novel *Trimalchio in West Egg*. Paradox or irony appears, also, in Jordan's observations, one of which she makes in her assessment of Gatsby's party. She likes large parties because "they're so intimate"; she explains, "At small parties there isn't any privacy." Additional comments later in the novel reinforce her incongruous, ironic observations about life.

Study Questions

1. What kinds of cars does Gatsby use to transport guests?

2. How do the guests behave?

3. What does Nick wear to the party?

4. How does Gatsby interact with the guests?

5. What observation does Owl-Eyes make about Gatsby's library?

6. What is Nick's first opinion of Gatsby?

7. What happens at the end of the party as the guests are leaving?

8. What does Gatsby's formal gesture of waving farewell remind us of?

9. What story does Nick recall about Jordan, and what is the catalyst for his remembering?

10. How does Nick provide a contrast, a foil character, to Jordan?

Answers

1. His station wagon and a Rolls-Royce provide transportation for the guests.

2. The guests display the rules of behavior associated with amusement parks.

3. He dresses up in his white flannels.

4. He does not participate.

5. The library contains real books though the pages have yet to be cut. Here, and in references to Tom's "reading," the emphasis seems to be on pseudo-intellectualism.

6. He is impressed with his smile and his genuine interest.

7. A wheel comes off a drunken guest's car, and the occupants end up in a ditch.

8. Earlier he extended his arm over the bay toward the green light.

9. She "had moved her ball from a bad lie in the semi-final round" of a golf tournament. Nick remembers this scandal as he and Jordan are "on a house-party together up in Warwick," and she leaves a borrowed car out in the rain with the top down, and then lied about it.

10. Jordan is "incurably dishonest"; Nick is exceedingly honest.

Suggested Essay Topics

1. Trace references to music in the Jazz Age—specific songs, types of instruments, description of the sounds—and draw a conclusion about their purpose(s). Discuss the dominant musical types of the 1920s.

2. Find a list of the seven deadly sins and the seven cardinal virtues. Write a paper in which you analyze some or all of the characters in regard to these sins and virtues. Which vice or virtue does each manifest?

3. Study Nick as a symbol of honesty and Jordan as a symbol of dishonesty. Write a character sketch which reveals their likenesses and differences in terms of veracity and credibility.

Chapter 4

New Character:

Meyer Wolfsheim: *a business connection of Gatsby's*

Summary

Another party takes place at Gatsby's mansion, this time on a Sunday morning. The narrator crowds an artist's canvas with his description of the guests, every possible type included, and thus creates vignettes of the time period. The chapter begins with a lengthy description of the guests, and it concludes, much as a periodic sentence does, with the summary: "All these people came to Gatsby's house in the summer." Nick records their names on a railroad timetable dated July 5, 1922. Young ladies at the party continue, even while guests of Gatsby, to whisper rumors about their host. All come to gamble and to drink, both illicit activities of the day. Yet no one is concerned about illegality.

One morning in late July, Gatsby unexpectedly picks up Nick for a drive to the city, his car a rich cream color, his suit caramel-colored. Inexplicably, he begins to reveal some of his story, swearing to tell Nick "God's truth." Born to wealthy parents in the

Middle West—all deceased now—he had been educated at Oxford and, after inheriting his family's wealth, had lived "like a young rajah" in Paris, Venice, and Rome, collecting rubies, dabbling in hunting, painting, trying to forget a sad experience, one of which he promises to share with Nick that afternoon. Because of this trauma, he wanted to die in the war, yet seemingly he bore "an enchanted life." He fought bravely and was promoted to major. He was eventually decorated for valor in war, including service rendered in Montenegro.

Speeding along, Gatsby's car is stopped by a policeman who, when Gatsby displays a white card from the commissioner, apologizes. Obviously, Gatsby had once "befriended" the commissioner, and the city official is indebted. A hearse and a limousine pass them as they proceed to the city. In a cellar restaurant on 42nd Street, Nick is introduced to Meyer Wolfsheim, a racketeer, who offers him a business "gonnection." Almost in the same breath he reminisces about a former "gonnection," Rosy Rosenthal, who had been gunned down, ostensibly by underworld connections. Gatsby prepares Nick for a meeting with Jordan, a plan established at Gatsby's earlier party, to accommodate a rendezvous with Daisy. When Tom appears in the same restaurant, Nick goes over to speak with him and to introduce Gatsby; but when he turns, Gatsby has disappeared.

That afternoon, Jordan recalls with nostalgia her 1917 friendship in Louisville with Daisy. Popular with young officers from Camp Taylor, Daisy had also spent some time with Gatsby, who, as a result, planned to marry her. Prevented by her mother from going to New York to say good-bye to him when he shipped out, she shortly thereafter met and married Tom Buchanan, whose $350,000 pearl necklace apparently surpassed the love she might have had for Gatsby.

Jordan, a bridesmaid in the wedding, fills in the details for Nick: after a three months' honeymoon to the South Seas, Tom was already having extramarital affairs. The next April Daisy had a daughter, Pammy. Despite moving with "a fast crowd," Daisy maintained a sterling reputation, perhaps "because she doesn't drink." Until six weeks before, she had not heard Gatsby's name again. By contrast, Gatsby had searched newspapers, hoping to

catch "a glimpse of Daisy's name." Nick responds sympathetically
to Jordan's account and agrees to provide his home as a place for
Gatsby and Daisy to be reunited. A phrase begins to beat in his
ears: "There are only the pursued, the pursuing, the busy, and the
tired." Gratified to have beside him a person, not a "disembodied
face" such as compelled Gatsby, Nick draws Jordan up closer,
tightening his arms. Her "wan, scornful mouth" smiles, and so he
draws her up again "closer," this time to his face.

Analysis

The same subjects and devices continue to develop in Chapter
4. References appear early in the chapter to bootlegging and illicit
sexual liaisons, even in the descriptions of the myriad of guests who
came to Gatsby's, perceived by the narrator as "the world and its
mistress." At least hinting of some criminal activity about to come
to light is the reference to Henry L. Palmetto, one of Gatsby's guests
who "killed himself by jumping in front of a subway train in Times

Square." A state senator participates in the bash even though prohibition was the law of the land. In listing guests from every social stratum, Nick, perhaps unwittingly, makes the point that society in general is corrupt. Everyone has a price. As the policeman rescinds the speeding ticket because of some connection with Gatsby, it seems clear that the commissioner can be bought. As Gatsby's grail begins to take shape in sordid reality, it seems clear that *anyone* can be bought. Where Myrtle can be bought with a simple dog collar, Daisy can be bought with a $350,000 pearl necklace. Entrepreneurs could pander to such tastes. Staggering as the idea is to Nick, even the 1919 World Series was "fixed," according to Gatsby, the work of one man—Meyer Wolfsheim.

More noticeable in this chapter are flower images. From the outset, of course, Daisy and Myrtle, as names of principal characters, subtly call attention to flowers, a daisy being a white flower with yellow at the center and myrtle, a shrub with white flowers and dark berries. Daisy calls Nick "a rose, an absolute rose" in Chapter 1. In Chapter 4, we meet Benny McClenahan's female friends; he brings four girls to Gatsby's parties, their last names either "the melodious names of flowers and months or the sterner ones of the great American capitalists"—an interesting juxtaposition of flowers and money. The dead man who passes in a hearse is "heaped with blooms" to conceal the death beneath. At Daisy's Louisville home, her family has "the largest of the lawns." Nature, particularly gardens and flowers, is ever important with the suggestions, archetypal as they are, of birth and death in nature, of the cycle of life.

Cars in this chapter become increasingly important. Gatsby's car, described like a god's chariot, is a "rich cream color, bright with nickel, swollen here and there in its monstrous length with triumphant hat-boxes and supper-boxes and tool-boxes, and terraced with a labyrinth of windshields that mirrored a dozen suns." Riding in it is like "sitting down behind many layers of glass in a sort of green leather conservatory." The diction emphasizes the mythological association, "labyrinth" suggesting the story in mythology of the minotaur, the windshields mirroring a dozen suns suggestive of Apollo, god of light, or Icarus, who flew too near the sun. Going through the Valley of Ashes, Gatsby's car has its "fenders spread like wings," another image which reinforces the demigod or godlike image. Ironically, Daisy drove a little white roadster, always preferring white, even at 18; equally ironic, the white pearls valued at $350,000 determined her choice of marriage partner. The return from the wedding trip finds Tom with a chambermaid in his car on the road to Ventura—he "ripped a front wheel off his car," an experience much like Owl-Eyes' earlier mishap. Even a hearse and a limousine are included in the exhibition of automobiles. The physically dead and the morally dying, the respectable and the less-than-respectable, come together both literally and thematically.

The objective correlative and the archetype appear here, as well. The song being sung by little girls in Central Park is "The Sheik of Araby," the lyrics of which tell of the sheik's creeping into the tent where the maiden is sleeping. Such songs evoke in the reader familiar with the melody or lyrics of this 1920s song a nostalgic re-action. Hearing the song even in imagination recalls the lifestyles, the dances, the appearance typical of the 1920s. Gatsby's car has a "three-noted horn," perhaps suggestive of a flourish of trumpets before the appearance of royalty.

The rumors about Gatsby persist in this chapter; even Gatsby is aware of them, a situation he tries to dispel by telling Nick his story, or the story as he wishes it were, believes that it was. Even he believes he has led a charmed life. Like a supernatural hero, a hero with mythical powers, he has survived war, rejection, unre-quited love; now he believes he can recapture and relive the past. The music, the bootlegged alcohol, the cars, the freedom females experienced—all of these contribute to the subliminal effect of the objective correlative. And for Nick, at least, Gatsby comes alive as the romantic American hero, "delivered suddenly from the womb of his purposeless splendor."

The drunk scene in which Daisy destroys a letter from Gatsby and then marries Tom the next day is central to understanding the irony of the novel. Although Daisy does not drink, the night she receives the note from Gatsby she drinks herself into a stupor; and after sobering up in a tub and succumbing to the influence of her mother, she decides to abandon Gatsby and marry Tom. Crucial to understanding the importance of this scene is the conventional resolution of the conflict between love and money. In the Horatio Alger stories, in rags-to-riches narratives, love wins out over money. In this instance, however, money wins. Daisy "sells out" without a shiver. Jordan speculates that "perhaps Daisy never went in for amour at all." Just as Myrtle "sells out" to have an affair with Tom, Daisy, in a higher caste of society, sells out, it seems, in return for a $350,000 necklace. Fitzgerald's point seems to be that if the price is right, everyone will succumb. Thus, the conventional motif of the American Dream is inverted. If the end is acquisition of money, any means are justified.

Study Questions

1. What is the date at this point in the novel?

2. Whom does Nick encounter at Gatsby's party?

3. What is the suggestion about Henry L. Palmetto's death?

4. In the description of Gatsby's car, what is the significance of its being bright with nickel and swollen in its monstrous length with all kinds of boxes?

5. What phrase does Gatsby repeatedly use to address Nick and others?

6. In what country did Gatsby receive a medal "For Valour Extraordinary"?

7. Who fixed the World Series in 1919, according to Gatsby?

8. Why is Daisy's reputation so pristine?

9. For how long has Gatsby been pursuing Daisy?

10. What phrase keeps coming back to Nick?

Answers

1. It is now July 5, 1922, and shortly thereafter.

2. Somewhat surprisingly, he runs into Jordan Baker.

3. It was a suicide prompted by some dark dealing or situation.

4. It is like a god's chariot.

5. He often calls others "Old Sport," a phrase he perhaps picked up while studying briefly at Oxford.

6. In tiny Montenegro he was recognized for valor.

7. According to Gatsby, the Series was fixed by one man—Wolfsheim, a fictional character based on a real person.

8. Daisy does not drink.

9. Gatsby has been reading papers, keeping clippings, looking tirelessly for Daisy for five years.

10. Nick remembers the saying, "There are only the pursued, the pursuing, the busy, and the tired."

Suggested Essay Topics

1. Show how the American Dream associated with America's past has succumbed to mercenary, almost exclusively materialistic values, derived from get-rich-quick schemes. Find evidence of the historical basis in fact and corresponding evidence in the novel.

2. Elaborate on the epigram: "There are only the pursued, the pursuing, the busy, and the tired." Show how it contributes to the development of plot, character, and theme in the novel. Give justification for its being the single most important line in the novel.

3. Determine where this chapter fits on the pyramid of dramatic structure: antecedent action (or what has taken place before the action of the novel begins), inciting moment (or the catalyst which creates interest in the actions and conflicts which follow), rising action (or the intensifying of interest and suspense), climax (or most intense moment from which there is no turning back for the protagonist), reversal (or falling action), and denouément (or tying up of loose ends). Defend your decision.

4. Select one or more of the names Nick lists on his timetable, and research to discover their stories and to comprehend Fitzgerald's choice of those names. How were they involved in American history?

5. Research Montenegro and discern its role in World War I. Gauge Gatsby's account of wartime activity by these historical findings.

Chapter 5

New Character:

Klipspringer: *the boarder at Gatsby's house*

Summary

Nick returns home at 2:00 in the morning to find Gatsby's house lit up "like the World's Fair." Gatsby is anxious concerning the meeting Nick is to orchestrate with Daisy, a long-awaited reunion. He invites Nick to go to Coney Island in his car or "take a plunge in the swimming pool," but his neighbor, who must work the next day, demurs, saying it's too late—he has to go to bed. This invitation to swim foreshadows the eventual demise of Gatsby.

Knowing or strongly suspicioning Nick's meager circumstances, Gatsby offers to "set him up in business"—it wouldn't take up much time, but he "might pick up a nice bit of money"—but then refuses to answer queries about the nature of the business, explaining it's "a rather confidential sort of thing." On the day agreed upon, Gatsby sends over a greenhouse of flowers and a tea service. At two minutes before the appointed time, he despairs and decides to go home. He decides that Daisy is not coming.

Of course, he is wrong. Awkward, difficult in many ways, the reunion reignites Daisy's fervor for Gatsby. When he reclines against the mantelpiece "in a strained counterfeit of perfect ease, even of boredom," he knocks a "defunct" clock off. Gatsby apologizes, saying, "I'm sorry about the clock." Nick assures him it is an old clock, a comment followed immediately by Daisy's saying, "We haven't met for many years," and Gatsby's replying, "Five years next November."

Together with Nick and Gatsby, she tours Gatsby's house, pausing to examine piles of shirts from Gatsby's closet. Daisy cries. Inadvertent comments and interrupting telephone calls inform Nick of Gatsby's business activities. When Nick asks Gatsby what business he is in, he impulsively retorts, "That's my affair." A picture of Dan Cody elicits an explanation of Cody's part in Gatsby's career. The clipped responses to one phone call—"I said a small town ... He must know what a small town is... Well, he's no use to us if Detroit is his idea of a small town"—are consistent with speculation and Gatsby's own comments about his being in the "drug business," possibly, as Tom will charge later, a front for bootlegging "grain alcohol" over the counter. Klipspringer, the "boarder," plays the piano at Gatsby's insistence; the songs he plays are "Ain't We Got Fun" and "The Love Nest." When Daisy calls Gatsby to look at the clouds following the rain, it is clear that he is bewildered, awestruck again by Daisy's voice, that voice, like the Sirens' of mythology, "a deathless song." Nick slips away down the marble steps, "leaving them there together."

Analysis

As the chapter begins, Gatsby realizes he is closer to attaining his dream, Daisy, than he has been for five years. Anxious and edgy, he admits to "a little business on the side," thinking Nick might want a "piece of the action." Gatsby now sees everything—his wardrobe, his furnishings, his home—through Daisy's eyes, and, understandably, wonders about their acceptability to her. Everything he has done, everything he has accumulated clearly is for her.

At Nick's bungalow, Gatsby is reunited with Daisy. The scene reiterates a sort of death of time. Like a child counting the days until Christmas, Gatsby has counted the days before he could start life over with Daisy. Gatsby cannot be convinced that it is impossible to repeat the past; it is crucial to him that he and Daisy be able to go back to their Louisville relationship. Because Gatsby now has the fortune he lacked before, Daisy can choose him, as she had chosen Tom for the same motivation before, and enjoy both love and affluence. Gatsby is haunted by time, and the references to it both here and in other chapters emphasize the angst he experiences and has experienced for five years. Strongly contributing to this theme of repeating the past, or at least attempting to, is Fitzgerald's manipulation of time. The novel does not develop sequentially and in a straightforward manner; rather, the reader sees and learns through Nick's eyes. The result is empathy with Gatsby and his idealism.

Both at the initial reunion and at the tossing into the air of Gatsby's shirts, Daisy cries. Moved by the show of prosperity, the dream girl responds as Gatsby would wish. This show of maudlin sentimentality parallels Myrtle's tearful response to returning George's borrowed wedding suit to its owner. It is unlike Gatsby to display wealth and possessions so ostentatiously. He continues to react and evaluate through Daisy's "well-loved" eyes.

Almost subconsciously, Gatsby admits his long pursuit of Daisy. He matter-of-factly states that she has a green light "that burns all night" at the end of her dock. Absorbed in the significance of that observation, he tacitly acknowledges that "the colossal significance of that light had now vanished forever," for the real Daisy, in contrast to the idealized Daisy, is no longer an "enchanted object." The enchantment had become his total being,

had consumed him—no human could have measured up. Daisy must have "tumbled short of his dreams—not through her own fault, but because of the colossal vitality of his illusion." Daisy's voice once again endears her: it is "a wild tonic in the rain" but at the same time, like the song of the sirens, it lures Gatsby to final destruction. Her voice "was a deathless song."

At the birth and passing and during the adventures of a mythic hero, the primitive elements—earth, air, fire, and water—appear. Again, Gatsby fits the mold. His created identity began with his introduction to high living through Dan Cody, a debauchee whose yacht provided for Gatsby the conveyance that transcended earth over water, just as Lancelot ascended to Heaven over water and bridges in Arthurian legend. On the day of this delayed epiphany, nature provides rain off and on throughout the day and into the night. And "no amount of fire," the narrator suggests, can threaten "what a man will store up in his ghostly heart." The "fluctuating, feverish warmth" of Daisy's voice helps provide the element of fire in Gatsby's experience. The macrocosm—the universe—was made from these four primitive elements. The microcosm—man—has them in him as well: from dust he was created, according to Genesis; his breathing and sighs constitute air in the body; temper and passion replicate fire in the macrocosm; and the blood flowing through the veins corresponds to the rivers in the universe. All the elements create the archetypal hero image in Gatsby.

Recurring motifs function in this chapter as well as before. Colors are regal: Gatsby's silver shirt and gold-colored tie, Daisy's brass buttons gleaming on her dress, Gatsby's toilet set of "pure dull gold," and "golden billow of foamy clouds above the sea." Shirts with "stripes and scrolls and plaids in coral and apple-green and lavender and faint orange, with monograms of Indian blue" and Daisy's "three-cornered lavender hat" expand the palette to include pastels. The flowers are lilacs, "dripping bare," the bedrooms "swathed in rose and lavender silk and vivid with new flowers." Observing the clouds after the rain, Daisy whispers she wants to "get one of those pink clouds" and put Gatsby in it to push him around.

Music appears here in the form of Klipspringer's piano playing. He plays several tunes, including "Ain't We Got Fun" and "The Love Nest." The objective correlative includes these tunes and dances reflective of the Age of Flappers and Jazz.

Study Questions

1. Why does Nick say Gatsby's house looks like the World's Fair?

2. How does Gatsby's gardener help prepare for Daisy's visit?

3. How does Gatsby dress for the rendezvous with Daisy?

4. Who is the Finn referred to in Chapter 5?

5. How long has it been since Daisy and Gatsby had seen each other?

6. What does Gatsby's maid do when leaning out a central bay window?

7. In what way are the various rooms in Gatsby's mansion described in historical terms?

8. Who was Gatsby's first benefactor?

9. What part does nature play in the rendezvous?

10. Who provides the musical background for the love scene?

Answers

1. It is so lit up late at night.

2. He cuts Nick's grass as well as Gatsby's.

3. He wears a white flannel suit, silver shirt, and gold-colored tie, accouterments fit for a god.

4. She is Nick's domestic help.

5. Gatsby has counted every minute for these five years they have been apart.

6. She spits, an incongruous action in such a setting.

7. The description includes Marie Antoinette music-rooms and Restoration salons, a sort of continental decor.

8. Dan Cody, who had made money from silver and gold fields, took him aboard his yacht.

9. It rains.

10. When Daisy and Gatsby are reunited, Klipspringer plays the piano.

Suggested Essay Topics

1. Consider ways in which Gatsby might be a counterpart to Don Quixote. Research the characteristics of this fictional Spanish dreamer, and write an essay in which you show their likenesses and, of course, differences.

2. Consider ways in which Tom Buchanan and George Wilson are alike, in that the wives of both men are capable of being lured away by another man. Therefore, both men, different as they are, are cuckolds (a Middle Ages term, defining men whose wives are unfaithful. In the legendary account, such husbands were said to grow horns, thus becoming monsters).

3. The reunion of Daisy and Gatsby, a rather sordid relationship, signals simultaneously the beginning and the end of Gatsby's dream and of his success. Justify this statement.

Chapter 6

Summary

About this time, suspicions concerning Gatsby grow to such an extent that an "ambitious young reporter" attempts to get a statement from Gatsby or some story about this mysterious man's notoriety. Stories circulating have to do with an "underground pipe-line to Canada." As a result of such rumors, Nick chooses, at this point in the flashback, to detail Gatsby's younger years, stories not recounted in chronological order.

Not people of means, as Gatsby had earlier told Nick, Gatsby's parents were "shiftless and unsuccessful farm people"; in truth, he had never accepted them as his parents at all but saw himself as a son of God: he sprang from "his Platonic conception of himself." He created an image, a persona which he wanted to become and set out to accomplish it. Along the way, by his own admission, he had taken advantage of "young virgins because they were ignorant" and of "others because they were hysterical about things" he took for granted.

At the age of 17, James Gatz, more or less a "beach bum," was introduced to an exciting career, a Bohemian life, at the invitation of Dan Cody. Cody had taken in the young Gatz, as Meyer Wolfsheim would do later, probably because of his winsome smile. Cody, at 50, was "a product of the Nevada silver fields, of the Yukon, of every rush for metal since seventy-five." A "pioneer debauchee," he had "brought back to the Eastern seaboard the savage violence of the

frontier brothel and saloon." As a result of seeing the trouble created by Cody's drunkenness while serving in his employ, Gatsby
drank little. As a mentor, Cody was flawed.

After this flashback digression to account for Gatsby's outlook,
a group of three on horseback—"Tom and a man named Sloane
and a pretty woman in a brown riding habit"—come by Gatsby's
house; they casually and insincerely invite Nick and Gatsby to join
them for a ride and dinner. Nick excuses himself; Gatsby prepares
to join them by car since he has no horse. Gatsby does not know
he is being insulted. In the meantime, Gatsby mentions, almost
aggressively, that he has known Tom's wife before, a comment

which creates question in Tom's mind. The following Saturday Tom accompanies Daisy to Gatsby's party. Nick notices a different, oppressive atmosphere, simply because Tom is present. Tom is contemptuous of the party—of the guests, of the host, of Daisy's desire to be there. He accuses Gatsby and his guests of being bootleggers, an accusation Daisy refutes. She insists that Gatsby simply owns drug stores. Yet, except for the "moving-picture director and his Star," even Daisy is "appalled" by the "raw vigor" of West Egg. Two worlds collide in this situation.

After the party, Gatsby makes clear to Nick he plans to relive the past; he expects Daisy to renounce her marriage and love for Tom and return to that moment of commitment, as he understood his and Daisy's relationship, in Louisville five years earlier. He is incredulous when Nick argues that no one can repeat the past. Of course you can, he argues. This is the idealism of youth. Gatsby wants to recover "something, some idea of himself" as a young military officer in uniform. Returning in his mind's eye to Daisy's street, he sees that the blocks of the sidewalks really form a ladder, and so he "mounted to a secret place above the trees" where he could "suck on the pap of life, gulp down the incomparable milk of wonder." At the moment he kisses Daisy, however, his unutterable vision is fleshed out, incarnated, and thus his mind can never "romp again like the mind of God." The intangible became tangible; divinity became flesh. Though she blossomed for him at the kiss, the limitation imposed by the kiss is irreversible. The chapter ends with Nick's struggling to remember a phrase, a "fragment of lost words," that he had heard "somewhere a long time ago." Unable to remember, his lips make no sound, and what he had "almost remembered was uncommunicable forever."

Analysis

Perhaps the phrase Nick tries to recall is the same one that Fitzgerald wrote about in another work: "France was a land; England was a people, but America, having about it that quality of the ideal, was harder to utter—it was the graves at Shiloh and the tired, drawn, nervous faces of its great men, and the country boys dying in the Argonne for a phrase that was empty before their bodies withered. It was a willingness of the heart."

As Gatsby became the new identity, the Platonic conception of himself, he envisioned himself achieving that uncorrupted vision toward which he had worked all these years. Ironically, the *means* to that end were corrupt, financial schemes espoused by Gatsby, ostensibly because of Cody and Wolfsheim's influence initially. His belief centered on "a promise that the rock of the world was founded securely on a fairy's wing." Material values are inextricably bound up with dreams. To that belief he gave unstintingly of himself. Thus, Nick concludes that, though Gatsby "represented everything for which he had unaffected scorn," there was "something gorgeous about him, some heightened sensitivity to the promises of life." His "extraordinary gift for hope," the likes of which Nick had never found in any other person, convinces him that Gatsby turned out all right in the end. It was the "foul dust" that "floated in the wake of his dreams" that caused his demise.

Seemingly, Gatsby never really accepted his mother and his father in North Dakota as his parents. As Nick earlier observed, he could have sprung from the swamps of Louisiana—or any other mysterious origin. As heroes in the archetypal mold do, he came from mystical, mysterious beginnings. His parents might just as well have found him abandoned, a foundling, on a mountainside where Oedipus was abandoned and found. He continues to grow into the archetypal image. Part of his enigma, his charisma, is the smile, one which he acquired early on: he learned that "people liked him when he smiled." Surely, Wolfsheim was enamored of that smile, and so Gatsby was a very desirable and subsequently successful "front man."

Motifs which recur in this chapter include color imagery, Daisy's voice tag, and subliminal music as objective correlative. "Gray" surfaces again in association with decadence or decay. The "pioneer debauchee" Dan Cody is described as a "gray, florid man" with a hard empty face. Daisy's fur collar, a "gray haze," stirs in the breeze. She whispers to Nick at the party to present a *green* card for a kiss in return; she offers Tom a little *gold* pencil to write down addresses of anyone who might appeal to him. She facetiously identifies a guest as the man "with the sort of *blue* nose." Gatsby points out to Daisy a gorgeous guest, an *orchid* of a woman sitting under a *white*-plum tree. Thus, colors continue to add to the same thematic tapestry as they have done in previous sections.

Again in this chapter, Daisy's voice plays "murmurous tricks in her throat," and she begins to sing "in a husky, rhythmic whisper, bringing out meaning in each word that it had never had before and would never have again." One of the songs is "Three O'Clock in the Morning."

Gatsby is ever closer to his dream and to its fulfillment. He argues emphatically that he can go back to the Louisville scenario of five years before and simply pick up where he and Daisy left off. Now, having amassed a fortune, conceivably one greater than Tom's, he fully believes Daisy will prefer him, will renounce Tom, and will marry him. Where before he had only his military uniform,

now he has "a man in England" who buys his clothes, sending over "a selection of things at the beginning of each season." He displays shirts of every fabric and description—"of sheer linen and thick silk and fine flannel." He can indeed provide for Daisy in the manner to which she is accustomed. Ever the dreamer, he cannot possibly imagine that she will refuse.

The imagery is almost Biblical: his mind can never "romp again like the mind of God" if he weds his "unutterable visions to her perishable breath." When he kisses her, "the incarnation," a term associated with epiphany, God in flesh revealed to man, is complete. In this context, Gatsby, reminiscent of Faust who makes a bargain with the devil, sacrifices divine characteristics for fleshly, sensual desires.

Study Questions

1. In what state did Gatsby grow up?
2. What was his real name?
3. What was Dan Cody's background?
4. Who was Ella Kaye?
5. How much was to have been Gatsby's inheritance from Cody?
6. Why did he not receive it?
7. What is the significance of the threesome not waiting for Gatsby?
8. Why was Daisy appalled at Gatsby's party?
9. How did Tom charge Gatsby with making his money?
10. In what season of the year had Gatsby met and kissed Daisy?

Answers

1. Gatsby was reared in North Dakota.
2. He was named James or Jimmy Gatz.
3. Apparently, he had made a fortune in metals from Nevada silver fields and gold in the Yukon.

4. Ella Kaye was Cody's mistress.

5. He was to receive $25,000.

6. Ella Kaye found a legal strategy to cut him out and inherit Cody's millions herself.

7. He does not understand that their invitation is superficial; in fact, he is being insulted without being aware of it.

8. The sophistication and restraint of the "secret society are missing." The vitality and simplicity of Gatsby's guests are virtually palpable, and Daisy is unappreciative.

9. Tom denounces Gatsby as a bootlegger.

10. He had known her in Louisville in the autumn of the year.

Suggested Essay Topics

1. Study the various parties and guests at the parties in order to construct a thesis and arguments that typify America and Americans at play in the 1920s. What do the parties reveal about these guests?

2. Consider all the meanings of Daisy's admiration for the movie director leaning over his wife. Does she see herself in that image? Is Fitzgerald simply magnifying film, a new medium in the 1920s?

3. Gatsby grew into adolescence after being introduced to a tawdry lifestyle on Dan Cody's yacht. Show how the boy on the yacht was ironically more worldly and realistic than the unrealistic adult gazing longingly at the green light.

4. In what ways can Nick be said to be the real hero of the story? Prove your answer.

5. Select a line or a passage about time and show its thematic significance.

Chapter 7

New Character:

Michaelis: *friend and comforter of George*

Summary

As curiosity peaks concerning Gatsby, the lights fail to go on one Saturday night. Visitors in automobiles stay a few minutes and leave. When Nick inquires about Gatsby's welfare, the "butler" allays his concerns. The next day Gatsby explains he has dismissed his servants in order to protect Daisy's reputation when she comes to visit him in the afternoons. He extends an invitation to Nick to join him and Jordan Baker for lunch at the Buchanans' the next day. Unbearably hot, the train and the passengers on it emit signals and warnings of temper and passion corresponding to the intense heat of the summertime. The situation on the train foreshadows the incident later in New York City in the hotel room.

At the Buchanans' house, Gatsby sees for the first time Pammy, a living, tangible result of the marriage Gatsby has been unwilling to accept. Then, despairing from boredom and unrelieved heat, Daisy suggests they go to town, she and Gatsby in Gatsby's car, Nick and Jordan with Tom in his car. At the garage in the Valley of Ashes, Tom stops for gasoline, promises to sell George a car which he can then resell for profit, and hears George say he has decided to take Myrtle away. George explains they want to go West, partly because he has just learned of "something funny" going on in Myrtle's life. Suddenly, Nick becomes aware of eyes watching, not just those of Dr. T. J. Eckleburg but of Myrtle as she observes the scene from the upstairs window; he discerns from her facial expression that she believes Jordan to be Tom's wife.

In the Plaza Hotel, nothing relieves the heat—open windows, cool drinks, or relaxation. To the sounds of the wedding march from below where someone's wedding nuptials are taking place, sounds of discord between Daisy and Tom appear. When Tom begins to interrogate Gatsby about his past and his business dealings, Gatsby rises to the occasion, thus justifying Nick's confidence in him. But when Gatsby tries to force Daisy's hand, proclaiming to Tom that she had never loved him, emotions erupt. Tom calls Gatsby a swindler, a racketeer, a bootlegger, at which point Daisy begins to draw "further and further into herself." Tom instructs Daisy to start home in Gatsby's car; the others will follow. Nick suddenly remembers this is his thirtieth birthday, a significant entrance into a world of "loneliness, a thinning list of single men to know, a thinning briefcase of enthusiasm, thinning hair."

Following a space which indicates a hiatus or gap in the chronological account, Nick explains that Michaelis has come over to try to comfort Wilson. In the continuing flashback, it becomes clear that Myrtle had run out into the dark toward "a big yellow car," a "death car," and that the car hit and killed Myrtle and then drove on without stopping. George grieves uncontrollably as witnesses describe what happened. Tom stops the car he is driving to ascertain what happened. Naturally he assumes Gatsby had killed Myrtle and, in cowardly fashion, had driven on.

Outside the Buchanans' house, Gatsby waits to protect Daisy from any danger that might erupt. Nick, at first contemptuous of Gatsby's apparent carelessness and callousness, discovers through an inadvertent slip in Gatsby's conversation, that Daisy had been driving the "death car." However, Gatsby will say he was. Unappreciative of his self-sacrificing protection of her, Daisy sits with Tom at a table of cold fried chicken and bottles of ale, preparing her safe retreat back into the insulated protection of the secret society. So Nick walks away to a waiting taxi and watches Gatsby stand "in the moonlight—watching over nothing."

Analysis

A satiric reference appears at the beginning of Chapter 7, when Gatsby is described in the image of Trimalchio, the protagonist in Petronius' *Satyricon*. The giver of lavish parties now hosts only romantic trysts with Daisy. Hence, the need for servants no longer exists, and some of Wolfsheim's acquaintances take over the tasks previously held by servants. The whole "caravansary," or staff of servants, has fallen down like a house of cards "at the disapproval in her eyes." For such an affair, servants may be released. The diction choice of "caravansary," an inn for caravans in Persia, furthers the image of the rich, indulgent Trimalchio and reinforces the satiric intent of the reference. Tutored and coached by corrupt mentors, Gatsby's ethereal dream had unwittingly become tainted.

Another recurring image in this section is heat. The weather is relentlessly hot. On the train to the Buchanans' for lunch, Nick observes that this particular day is "the warmest day of the summer": it was "broiling." Straw seats "hovered on the edge of combustion," and the woman sitting next to him "lapsed despairingly into deep heat with a desolate cry." The conductor complains about the heat, an observation Nick follows with the fragmented and sardonic commentary, "That any one should care in this heat whose flushed lips he kissed, whose head made damp the pajama pocket over his heart!" Stated overtly is the association between the heat of the summer in the macrocosm and the heat of passion in the microcosm, an emphasis which continues in the action of this chapter. The physical heat of the sweltering last day of summer is no more intense than the fiery emotions—temper, passion, jealousy—of the characters. Ironically, both Jordan and Daisy look cool, as does Pammy, who comes in to be exhibited for the guests. Jordan reacts to Daisy's cynical boredom, exhorting her not to be morbid and wryly suggesting that "life starts all over again when it gets crisp in the fall," an atypical, inverted description of the archetypal fall of the year.

Bored, but, ironically, on the verge of the most intense, demanding crisis of her life, Daisy asks, "What'll we do with ourselves this afternoon and the day after that, and the next thirty years?" This rather existential assessment of life replicates or at least echoes the sentiment in T. S. Eliot's *The Wasteland*, a poem which influenced Fitzgerald significantly. She vacantly points out that Gatsby looks self-assured and cool even in his suit, a marked contrast with the rest of the scene. When Nick mentions Daisy's indiscreet voice, Gatsby matter-of-factly returns, it's "full of money." In this observation the tag Fitzgerald repeatedly uses in his identification of Daisy—her low voice—unites with the motivating force in her life, money, seemingly a motivation Gatsby has quietly understood and accepted.

Cars are exceedingly important in this chapter. That Daisy openly prefers riding with Gatsby shocks and appalls Tom, but he acquiesces, insisting that they drive his coupé while he, together with Nick and Jordan, will drive Gatsby's yellow open car with standard shift. When they stop for gas at George's garage, Myrtle sees from the upper window and assumes that Jordan, riding with Tom, is his wife. Cynically, Tom allows George to think he can buy Gatsby's car; he is, thus, led to believe that the car belongs to Tom.

While there, Gatsby and Daisy speed by in the blue coupé, and the threesome hurry along "toward Astoria at fifty miles an hour" to catch up with the "easy-going" blue coupé. On the return trip, however, Daisy and Gatsby drive the big yellow car, "the 'death car' as the newspapers called it," a fact that leads George ultimately to seek information from Tom about the owner/driver. Nick's statement, "So we drove on toward death through the cooling twilight," expresses not just the literal truth of the experience but the thematic point as well—the car, a symbol of the driving quality, the recklessness of these people. They could destroy the lives of others and then simply retreat into their money.

The images of cars also reflect the restless, driving nature of the characters. This restless, driving nature appears tangibly in the repeated images of cars. To notice the kind of car the characters drive is to perceive his or her character. Nick's "old Dodge" is the first of such automobiles mentioned. Daisy drives a white road-ster; Gatsby, one of "monstrous length" with "fenders spread like wings," a "rich cream color," the interior "a sort of green leather conservatory." Tom drives a conservative blue coupé; Jordan bor-rows her aunt's convertible and leaves the top down one rainy day. In George's garage is a "dust-covered wreck of a Ford." Recurring words, such as *restless, brooding,* and *driving,* reinforce the depic-tion of a restless American society in the 1920s.

In the hotel room, as Tom charges Gatsby with various crimi-nal activities, Daisy begins her metamorphosis. Gatsby's extreme wealth starts to lose its appeal as she starts to believe Tom's ac-cusations. Gatsby, "a common swindler," "a bootlegger," and a conspirator in some new scheme that Tom's sleuth, Walter Chase, is "afraid" to tell about, loses luster in her eyes; still, Gatsby inno-cently, naïvely believes Daisy will denounce Tom and her marriage to return to him and the love they had experienced five years before.

Color images again proliferate in this chapter. New York City, symbolically through cream colors, comes a little closer to the golden world and lifestyle of the rich. Gold and shades of gold—cream, caramel-colored, yellow—are dual in meaning. Clearly, they pertain to wealth and opulence, but they also associate with waste and decadence and cowardice. In this case, gold represents a sellout of America's idealism and true character, at least as it was originally perceived.

Eyes, as a pattern of imagery, are noticeable. To emphasize seeing, perceiving, understanding, Fitzgerald uses a plethora of eye images. Daisy's eyes, Gatsby fears, will reflect disapproval; in fact, they reflect fascination, at least initially. They look at Tom frowningly, yet later, in the hotel room, she looks at Gatsby out of "frightened eyes." Tom's eyes are flashing, and he claims to have a second sight. Dr. T. J. Eckleburg's faded eyes "keep their vigil," and George," hollow-eyed," shades his eyes. Myrtle's eyes have peculiar intensity and are wide with jealous terror when she sees the party headed for New York City.

Perhaps the most significant device in this chapter is the final image. Nick walks away from Gatsby, who is anxious that Tom might find out that Daisy had been driving. Nick leaves Gatsby "standing there in the moonlight—watching over nothing." The image clearly recalls the one at the end of Chapter 1 where Gatsby watches over the green light at the end of Daisy's dock. By juxtaposing the two images, the purpose becomes clear: as a goal, as the tangible American Dream, Daisy is inadequate, unworthy. The dreamer has invested everything to attain her; now, the narrator tells us, looking at her is like "—watching over nothing." As an obsessive pursuit, she is unworthy. By revisiting this image and by calling attention to the difference in the two scenes, just by using the dash to denote a breaking off, a device to slow the reader down and thus emphasize the changed interpretation, Nick as narrator subtly conveys his assessment of the situation and, beyond the actual incident, of the broader American Dream.

Study Questions

1. Why does Gatsby let all his domestic help go?

2. Whom does he use instead?

3. Why do the characters decide to go to New York?

4. What does Pammy wear when she comes into the room?

5. What does Gatsby say about Daisy's voice?

6. What does Tom drive to New York?

7. Who rides with Gatsby?

8. What comment does Tom make about drug stores?

9. Of what does Tom accuse Gatsby?

10. How old is Nick at the party?

Answers

1. He dismisses them to accommodate meetings with Daisy and her wish for privacy.

2. He uses connections of Wolfsheim's, people who owed him favors.

3. They want to escape the heat and boredom.

4. Like her mother, she wears white.

5. Her voice is "full of money."

6. He drives Gatsby's yellow car.

7. Only Daisy rides with Gatsby.

8. You can buy gasoline or most anything else at such stores—even liquor, he implies.

9. He accuses him of bootlegging, gambling, swindling, and even something bigger and more damaging than these.

10. Nick turns 30 years old on this day.

Suggested Essay Topics

1. Write an essay analyzing the Gatsby-Trimalchio connection and its importance. Compare Trimalchio, the hero or protagonist of *The Satyricon*, to Gatsby. Refer to William Rose Benét's *The Reader's Encyclopedia* for concise background information.

2. Trace the recurring image of eyes, and ascertain the purposes of those images. Consider blindness on any level as well as sight.

3. Compare the two passages below from T. S. Eliot's *The Wasteland* with remarkably similar ones from *The Great*

Gatsby. Better still, find a copy of the poem and discover other passages which correspond. What do the similarities suggest?

"I think we are in rats' alley
Where the dead men lost their bones..."

"What shall I do now? What shall I do?
I shall rush out as I am, and walk the street
With my hair down, so, What shall we do tomorrow?"

and from *Gatsby*, Chapter 2:

"It seemed to me that the thing for Daisy to do was to rush out of the house, child in arms—but apparently there were no such intentions in her head."

and from Chapter 7:

"What'll we do with ourselves this afternoon?" cried Daisy, "and the day after that, and the next thirty years?"

4. Explain the significance of the comments: "They weren't happy...and yet they weren't unhappy either. There was an unmistakable air of natural intimacy about the picture, and anybody would have said that they were conspiring together."

Chapter 8

Summary

Nick's restlessness precludes sleep. When he hears Gatsby return home in a taxi, he rushes over, feeling he should warn his neighbor to go away for a while, knowing the car will be traced. Aghast, Gatsby explains that he has to stay to protect Daisy, the first "nice" girl he has ever known. He uses Nick's visit as an opportunity to relive the Dan Cody story and his Camp Taylor experience.

Like many other officers, Gatsby had visited Daisy while in Louisville, but always he knew he was in her beautiful house by a "colossal accident." Again, like many others, "Gatsby took Daisy one still October night" because "he had no real right to touch her hand." Ever since that time, she had been his grail. She had disappeared into her rich house, much as she now retreats into the secret society, but he felt he must one day marry her because of what had transpired between them. Gatsby was surprised to find that he loved Daisy.

Abroad, Gatsby did well in the war; but instead of being shipped back home, he was sent to Oxford. Young and restless, Daisy was losing confidence in their relationship, and so she began going out again, "half a dozen dates a day with half a dozen men." When Gatsby did get back home, Daisy and Tom were on their wedding trip. He stayed a week in Louisville, spending the last of his army pay.

Back in the present, morning comes, and the gardener, the last of Gatsby's servants, comes to say he is planning to drain the pool, autumn being in the air. Gatsby suggests he wait since he himself had not used the pool all summer. Ironically, unaware that Daisy and Tom are already packing their bags for an escape abroad, he waits for Daisy's call, not the usual calls from Chicago or Philadelphia or Detroit, while floating on an air mattress in the pool he had not used before. When Nick leaves for work, he shouts, "They're a rotten crowd. You're worth the whole damn bunch put together."

At work Jordan telephones Nick, but he fails to establish any future plans for seeing her. He is unable to reach Gatsby by phone because the line continues to be busy, perhaps being held for incoming "business" calls or, more likely, a call from Daisy. Nick plans to take the 3:50 train home.

The narrative then takes us back to the Valley of Ashes where, the night before, Michaelis continued to befriend George. He asks if he and Myrtle had ever had children. George explains he has found a dog leash wrapped in tissue paper on her bureau: they have no dog. As he grieves, he looks out the window at the eyes of Dr. T. J. Eckleburg. He remembers telling Myrtle, "God knows what you've been doing." Still looking at the billboard, he also recalls warning, "God sees everything." Seeing George's eyes fixed on the billboard, Michaelis simplistically reminds him, "That's an advertisement." Michaelis leaves at 6:00, relieved by another watcher, but then George leaves, stops for a sandwich, which he does not eat, and a cup of coffee; and for three hours disappears from view. By 2:30 he has found out what he needed to know about the owner of the death car and is asking someone the way to Gatsby's house. By now, he knows Gatsby's identity. Thirty minutes before, Gatsby had entered the pool; no telephone message arrived. Surreptitiously, George glides toward Gatsby, fires a gun killing him, and then turns the gun on himself. "And the holocaust was complete."

Analysis

By this stage of the novel, the literary techniques, noted already, begin to coalesce to clarify and emphasize themes. Auditory and color images, cars and eyes as symbols, recurring tags to characterize—these and other devices reinforce Fitzgerald's statement concerning the American Dream. Sounds or auditory images appear early. At the beginning of the chapter, Nick hears a "groaning foghorn," a subtle reminder of the physical manifestation of Gatsby's dream—the green light across the bay. Another 1920s song surfaces in the flashback to Daisy and Gatsby's first meeting in Louisville, this time the *Beale Street Blues*, always, it seems, accompanied by the wail of the saxophone. Such is the objective correlative. The ringing of the telephone in Nick's office, described like "a divot from a green golf-links," seems to come sailing in the window; it is a call from Jordan. The telephone, too, connects characters with some of the baser elements of society. Gatsby receives frequent phone calls ostensibly from his underworld connections. Tom receives calls from his mistress, even during dinner in his own home. Ultimately, the shots fired to end Gatsby's life are heard by the chauffeur, "one of Wolfsheim's protégés." Combined, the sounds intensify and connect with the wail, the lament of wasted lives.

Colors contrast significantly in this section of the palette. In Daisy's girlhood home, romances were not laid away in lavender but were gay and radiant. In fact, her world was "redolent of orchids." Dancing went on all night; a "hundred pairs of golden and silver slippers shuffled the shining dust," and at the "gray tea hour" there were rooms with fresh faces, coming and going, drifting here and there "like rose petals blown by the sad horns around the floor." Daisy was fresh with "many clothes," the golden girl, the king's daughter, "gleaming like silver, safe and proud above the hot struggles of the poor," always remembered driving her white car. Sad and disillusioned, Gatsby leaves Louisville on a yellow trolley. Brought back into the present by the dawn, Nick notices light filling the house with "gray-turning, gold-turning light," a description with symbolic overtones. Nick compliments Gatsby, who is standing on his doorsteps, waving good-bye in his "gorgeous pink rag of a suit," a bright spot of color against the white steps. Tenacious in hope, Gatsby maintains his "romantic readiness" to the very end. In retrospect, Nick is glad he paid Gatsby the compliment that he was worth more than the whole "rotten crowd" put together.

In the Valley of Ashes as Michaelis tries to console George and assuage his grief, "hard brown beetles kept thudding against the dull light," and George shows Michaelis the dog-leash "made of leather and braided silver." As Wilson turns his eyes to the ash-heaps, "small gray clouds took on fantastic shapes and scurried here and there in the faint dawn wind." The yellow death car and the yellowing trees combine to portend death for the driver of the car and, simultaneously, for the season of the year, aided by the "ashen, fantastic figure gliding" toward Gatsby through the amorphous trees, leaving his mark in "a thin red circle" of blood in the water. The spectrum of colors—at times the connotation clear, at other times dual or ambivalent—subtly but effectively delineates the difference between a dream in its pure state and the perversion of that dream, "foul dust" floating in the wake of it.

An interesting and significant allusion appears in Chapter 8, a reference which helps to clarify Gatsby's dream quality. Having "taken" Daisy, Gatsby felt an obligation to marry her, a responsibility which subsequently turned to love, much to his surprise. He found that "he had committed himself to the following of a grail." Like Galahad, the pure, sinless knight in Arthurian legend, Gatsby was pure, untainted by wealth, and wedded to the vision of this damsel on high. He forsakes all to pursue the grail. He pays any price to win this most valuable person. Ironically, Daisy is unworthy as a quest. Although she is described as the only nice girl Gatsby had ever known, Fitzgerald puts the word *nice* in quotation marks. Once again, the punctuation enables the novelist to explain his meaning. Ultimately, Gatsby's body ends up on the floor of the pool, corresponding in an inverted way to the passing of Galahad from this life, his passing associated with water but in an inverted, upside-down way. Realistically, she could not have risen to the stature expected; perhaps it was unfair of Gatsby to expect it of her.

Again in Chapter 8, the craftsman/novelist continues the epithet-like descriptions. Daisy's voice is "huskier and more charming than ever," the recurring tag associated with her voice characterizing her as charming and rich, commanding and demanding. Keeping half a dozen dates a day with half a dozen men, she was living in a "twilight universe," one that would make Nick's provincial squeamishness, his inherent honesty, most uncomfortable. Gatsby, though, smiles his "radiant and understanding smile," a part of the tag characterization that recurs. His smile has "a quality of eternal reassurance in it." It understands you as far as you want to be understood, believes in you as you would like to believe in yourself, and assures you that it has precisely the impression of you that, at your best, you hope to convey. He typifies the quintessential friend. He waved Nick good-bye as he had signaled many other guests over the past five years. From them he had concealed his "incorruptible dream."

Toward the end, dust descriptions intensify. Little boys in the Valley of Ashes are looking for "dark spots in the dust," and Wilson observes "small gray clouds" which take on "fantastic shapes." He himself becomes one of those shapes as he approaches Gatsby's house: he is an "ashen, fantastic figure," gliding through amorphous trees. Conversely, garden images diminish. Gatsby acknowledges how "grotesque" a thing a rose is, and he probably concludes that he has paid "a high price for living too long with a single dream." Dust and ashes make the statement that America, like this individual product of its conditioning, has paid too high a price to achieve the traditional, undefiled dream.

Naming, another literary technique, provides the same commentary. The title of the book, *The Great Gatsby*, deserves attention. Is Gatsby truly great? Is he the epitome of the American Dream? After all, he is a bootlegger, a man with unsavory underworld connections, a fraud in the sense that he misrepresents his origin. Does *Gatsby* derive from *gat*, the term for *gun* popular in the 1920s? Since

Gatsby presents himself as "a son of God" who must be about his father's business, it is *possible* that the title is meant to suggest "God's boy," a phrase which means just that—"he must be about His Father's business." This description alludes to Jesus, who in New Testament accounts explains an absence to his earthly parents by saying he was in the temple—they should have known where to find him, for he had to be about His Father's business. Nick's interpretation of that business in Gatsby's case is "the service of a vast, vulgar, and meretricious beauty"—such as wealth. Such a Platonic conception is the kind of creation a 17-year-old boy "would be likely to invent, and to this conception he was faithful to the end." Seeing himself as a god or demigod, perhaps bearing a charmed life, he steadfastly continues on his quest for what he perceives to be the highest good. Had Fitzgerald stayed with his original title, *Trimalchio of West Egg,* he would have made a statement in that way as well. If Gatsby is like Trimalchio, a vulgar and obscenely rich protagonist, the purpose is clear. These are pejorative designations. If he as a product of the American Dream is the best America can produce, the novel is indeed a tragedy.

Other names equally important include Daisy, a flower that is associated with daybreak; the word originally meant "day's eye." The break of day should be a harbinger of newness, freshness, purity; ironically, Daisy, "gleaming like silver, safe and proud above the hot struggles of the poor," cynical and bored, is quite the opposite. Names of settings—East and West *Egg,* associated with birth and new life, and the Valley of Ashes, associated with death and waste and, by extension, "the valley of the shadow of death"—function significantly, too.

Thus, all the literary devices coalesce to reinforce and clarify the dominant theme—that we have wasted our potential, the original American Dream. The symbols, especially the eyes on the billboard and the green light, emphasize the contrast between the original untainted dream under the watchful eyes of a benevolent if omniscient God and the "Money-is-Everything" society where God has either forgotten about His creation or has turned His back upon it. Cars as symbols no less effectively convey the potential being replaced by the sordid. Images of colors and of heat as well as characterization carry the same message concerning the schism between the dream and reality in the American wasteland.

Study Questions

1. How late does Gatsby stand outside Daisy's house, waiting to see if she needed him?

2. Why is Gatsby's house unkempt?

3. Why does Nick advise Gatsby to go away a while?

4. Where had Gatsby met Daisy, according to the story he tells Nick?

5. What might Fitzgerald mean in describing Daisy's porch as "bright with the bought luxury of starshine"?

6. Why didn't Gatsby return to Daisy immediately after the war?

7. When Gatsby returned to Louisville, where was Daisy?

8. Why is the chauffeur about to drain the pool?

9. Why does Gatsby ask him to wait?

10. After learning who owns the yellow death car, what does Wilson do?

Answers

1. He waits until 4:00 a.m.

2. He has released all of his servants.

3. Nick is confident the car will be traced to Gatsby, putting Gatsby's life in jeopardy.

4. He met her while he was at Camp Taylor from which he and other officers went to visit Daisy.

5. The brightness in her description results from somebody's materialism.

6. He was sent to study at Oxford.

7. She was on her wedding trip with Tom.

8. With autumn approaching, leaves will fall and clog up the pipes.

9. He plans to take his first swim of the season in it.

10. Wilson kills Gatsby and then turns the gun on himself.

Suggested Essay Topics

1. Some of the characters in the novel symbolize a production ethic; others symbolize a consumption ethic. Classify the characters accordingly, and draw a conclusion about the American Dream, as you understand it, from Fitzgerald.

2. Eyes and sight recur frequently in the novel. What is Fitzgerald's statement about the ability to distinguish between illusion and reality?

3. How is this story an ironic inversion of a knightly quest for the grail?

Chapter 9

New Character:

Henry C. Gatz: *Gatsby's father who comes to attend the funeral*

Summary

Two years later, Nick remembers vividly the endless questioning by policemen and newspapermen in the wake of Gatsby's murder. Wilson, thought to be a madman, "a man deranged by grief," is found guilty, and the case is closed. When Nick calls Daisy, he learns that she and Tom have left with baggage, no destination or return date known. Subsequent calls to Wolfsheim and other "friends" are futile: no one can attend Gatsby's funeral. Three days later Henry Gatz sends a telegram with instructions to postpone the funeral until he can get there.

Bundled up against the September day, Mr. Gatz arrives and begins to exult in Gatsby's possessions. He brings with him an old picture, dirty and cracked, of Gatsby's house, and he shares the information that Gatsby had bought a house for him two years before. He produces a copy of *Hopalong Cassidy* in which Jimmy, as he was known as a boy, had written his daily schedule and "general resolves." Clearly, the boy had from childhood aspired to great plans, whatever they might be.

After waiting a long while, it becomes clear that nobody is coming to the funeral. After all the hundreds of guests that had come to Gatsby's house, no one cares enough or is too fearful to attend the funeral except Nick, Mr. Gatz, the minister, four or five servants, and the postman from West Egg. As they start into the cemetery, Owl-Eyes drives up. His eulogy—"The poor son-of-a-bitch"—succinctly sums up the situation. Of course, Daisy has not sent a message or flowers.

Nick's final visit with Jordan provides the opportunity for her to retort meaningfully that Nick, like her, had been a "bad driver."

He concludes he is 30 and too old to lie to himself and call it honor. One afternoon late in October he sees Tom Buchanan on Fifth Avenue. When Tom extends his hand, Nick refuses to shake it. Instead, he asks, almost rhetorically, "What did you say to Wilson that afternoon?" Tom acknowledges that he told him who owned the death car and then accuses Nick of having been duped by Gatsby, as Daisy had been earlier. He shares with Nick that he cried like a baby when he saw the box of dog biscuits in the flat he and Myrtle had shared. Nick concludes that "they were careless people," for they "smashed up things and creatures and then retreated back into their money or their vast carelessness, or whatever it was that kept them together, and let other people clean up the mess they had made."

Nick packs his trunk, returns for one last look at Gatsby's mansion, and returns to his Midwest. He philosophizes that this has been a story of the West, after all, and those in the East will be glad to be rid of his "provincial squeamishness." Belatedly, he becomes aware of the Dutch sailors who came to the new world in quest of a dream. Brooding on the old world, Nick thinks of Gatsby, wondering when he first picked out the green light. His dream must have seemed so close when, in actuality, it was already behind him. He promises that tomorrow we will run faster to attain that dream. Like boats, "we are borne back ceaselessly into the past."

Analysis

In this last chapter Nick enjoys the vantage point of two years as he looks back on the aftermath of Gatsby's death. Seemingly the closest person to his neighbor, Nick takes charge as best he can. Concurrent with the pathos of his reporting of the event and his taking Gatsby's side is the satiric commentary that a Gatsby is the best America can produce. As he tries to muster a crowd for the funeral, Nick makes indefatigable attempts by phone, by letter, and by visit to Wolfsheim. Ultimately, the day of the funeral, he visits Wolfsheim's office which is labeled "Swastika Holding Company." Inside, he hears someone whistling "The Rosary," tunelessly. For such a sinister man, an underworld character who wears cuff buttons made of the "finest specimens of human molars," it is ironic that he is whistling a religious tune.

Wolfsheim recalls that when Gatsby came out of the army he "was so hard up he had to keep on wearing his uniform because he couldn't buy some regular clothes." Like George who had to borrow a suit to be married in, Gatsby had to depend on a Wolfsheim to clothe and feed him, a gesture not altogether altruistic, since he saw in Gatsby's winsome smile and in his Oxford experience a front man without peer. Therefore, he "raised him up out of nothing, right out of the gutter." Nick has to wonder if their partnership had included the World Series transaction in 1919.

Another interesting facet of Gatsby's development is his book of schedules. Mr. Gatz finds it in a copy of *Hopalong Cassidy*, another name reference to the Old West, coincidentally the repository for Gatsby—or Jimmy's—early dreams. The list, which in some ways suggests Myrtle's list of "things to buy" in New York, includes the Ben Franklin virtues as found in his *Autobiography*. Gatsby's day began at an early 6:00 for exercise, study, work, sports, elocution, and poise as well as general resolves such as "saving $3.00 per week" and "being better to parents." These worthwhile albeit pathetic resolutions replicate, in part, the seven cardinal virtues, obviously worthy ideals for self-improvement. Regrettably, his goals to improve his mind, specifically, had been converted to goals concerning opulence and a hedonistic lifestyle when he met Dan Cody.

The eyes of the otherwise-anonymous Owl-Eyes now seem to suggest wisdom, despite his earlier inebriation. Having known Gatsby's situation, he concludes, "The poor son-of-a-bitch,"—the only, or at least the kindest, eulogy Gatsby would receive. Nick somberly synthesizes the situation and concludes, "This has been a story of the West, after all." Of note is his seeming condemnation of the mess we have made of the Western world discovered by breathless Dutch sailors centuries before. As he gazes at West Egg, especially, Nick sees a night scene by El Greco, a typical distortion of reality, of "a hundred houses, at once conventional and grotesque, crouching under a sullen, overhanging sky and a lustreless moon."

One last meeting with Jordan, her jauntiness still apparent, her balancing act with raised chin, her hair the color of an autumn leaf, convinces Nick this lifestyle is not for him. Perhaps she is right when she reminds him of his having said a bad driver was safe until she meets another bad driver. Nevertheless, Nick determines he is too far along, being 30, to play games and call it honor.

One last visit transpires with Tom, whom Nick encounters on Fifth Avenue. Tom has no problem admitting his involvement with identifying Gatsby as the driver of the car that killed Myrtle, a statement that verifies he still does not know Daisy was driving. He weeps, not because he caused Gatsby's murder for all practical purposes or had any involvement in that situation, but because the dog biscuits in the flat made him realize how awful it was to lose his mistress. George had likewise wept because of his love for Myrtle. The two men have one thing in common—as Myrtle was unfaithful to George, Daisy was unfaithful to Tom. Myrtle had called George a coward, but in the end he has enough courage to try to make amends for her death.

Tom, by contrast, cannot or will not accept the consequences of his actions. In the final judgment he *is* a coward. Nick recognizes the fact that Tom has no remorse, just as he had none at the time of the car wreck with the hotel maid while he and Daisy were virtually on their honeymoon. Tom finds a retreat into the world of money or vast carelessness, or "whatever it was that kept" him and Daisy together and "let other people clean up the mess they had made." They seem to live in the unending moral adolescence which only affluence can produce and protect. On all levels, morals are corrupt: if Daisy and Catherine and Myrtle can be bought, Fitzgerald must be saying that every man (or woman) has his (or her) price.

So Nick goes back home, taking the remnants of his "provincial squeamishness" out of Tom, Daisy, and Jordan's lives. One last look at Gatsby's house shows on the white steps "an obscene word, scrawled by some boy with a piece of brick." Nick erases it, drawing his shoe "raspingly along the stone." He remembers the "green breast of the new world" in connection with Gatsby and concludes they were "face to face for the last time in history with something commensurate to his capacity for wonder." That was the last "transitory enchanted moment" when man "must have held his breath in the presence of this continent, compelled into an aesthetic contemplation he neither understood nor desired." So goes the American Dream. Gatsby's dream was actually behind him "somewhere back in that vast obscurity beyond the city, where the dark fields of the republic rolled on under the night." The national dream, like Gatsby's in all its idealism, asked too much. Yet his spirit never succumbed. Nick's conclusion is that "we beat on, boats against the current, borne back ceaselessly into the past," even as he has relived the past as promised at the beginning of Chapter 1. Gatsby belongs to the past, not the future. Worthy of note is the fact that these final words are the epitaph on Fitzgerald's tombstone.

Still, Gatsby's green light was both his yesterday and his to-

morrow. It symbolized the dream of his boyhood and the hope of fulfillment in the future. It represents the reckless, success at any cost, pursuit of the entire American Dream. Nick describes it as representing "the orgiastic future that year by year recedes before us." It can be associated with the "green breast of the new world" in the most idealistic interpretation. As Daisy blossoms for Gatsby, the new world had flowered for the Dutch settlers. In the style of T. S. Eliot, he declares of the Dream, "It eluded us then, but that's no matter—tomorrow we will run faster, stretch out our arms farther...And one fine morning..."

Enough satirical devices are operative in the novel to justify calling it a satire. Conventional, universal symbols are inverted: white represents loss of purity; green below the surface suggests decadence or immorality. Silver and gold are immoral because of the price paid to acquire them. Names are ironic: the title, names of characters, names of guests written on the railroad schedule, such as the Leeches, the Catlips, the Dancies, and "Rotgut" Ferret, satirize the society of the 1920s.

Plot details are ironic: no moral differences exist in place or character, Fitzgerald seems to say. Settings are ironic: neither East Egg with its glittering mansions nor West Egg with its *nouveau riche* is worthy of imitation. The Valley of Ashes is certainly not desirable. Archetypal symbols are ironic: instead of spring being a time of new life, Jordan declares new life begins in the fall. Images of eyes suggest not God's looking over his universe but the *absence* of God. If He exists, his eyes, like Dr. T. J. Eckleburg's, are faded, enervated—He lacks concern. Materialism has replaced idealism, and neither has succeeded in accomplishing the true American Dream.

Nick is able to see what has happened to America from the Dutch sailors to Gatsby's world, and, though he has just turned 30, he is prepared and eager to return to the Midwest, leaving behind all the sophistication and superficiality, the "racy adventurous feel of it" that he initially enjoyed. He has no choice but to return to the environment where he learned human decencies and honor; his increasing awareness demands that he reject Jordan and the lifestyle she represents.

In the end, everyone's dreams are unfulfilled. Neither Nick's moralism, Gatsby's idealism, Tom's materialism, nor George's emotionalism produces gratification. The harshness of reality makes the American Dream futile; sadly, no one can return to the dreams of youth after maturity imposes that reality. No less clear is the comment that a nation has the same limitation.

As Daisy said at her daughter's birth, the best thing a girl can be is a beautiful fool. The shrines of the American Dream are beauty and appearance, self-adulation, money, and pleasure. These things are palpable; idealism is not. As satire, *The Great Gatsby* negates the American Dream.

Study Questions

1. How is Gatsby's death explained by the press in local newspapers?

2. How does Catherine respond to questions about her sister?

3. How does Wolfsheim's letter attempt to explain his not attending the funeral?

4. Who is Henry C. Gatz?

5. Why does Klipspringer call?

6. When Nick locates Wolfsheim's office and demands to see him, what is ironic about the situation?

7. How does Wolfsheim remember Gatsby?

8. Why did Gatsby continue to wear Army uniforms?

9. What could Nick mean when he concludes, "This has been a story of the West, after all—"?

10. What is the meaning of the last paragraph, the metaphor, of the book?

Answers

1. Wilson is a "madman," reduced to a "man deranged by grief."

2. She declares she has never known Gatsby, that she was "completely happy with her husband," and that she has never been involved in any kind of mischief.

3. He is tied up in important business and cannot "get mixed up in this thing now."

4. He is Gatsby's father from Minnesota.

5. He calls about some shoes he left at Gatsby's, not out of concern.

6. Wolfsheim is sinister and apparently ruthless, but he is whistling "The Rosary."

7. He was a major, just coming out of the army, covered with medals.

8. He was so poor he could not afford regular clothes.

9. It is the story of the Western continent as well as the Midwest contrasted with the East.

10. We persist in our drive forward, but, like boats moving against the current, we are always borne back into the past. As the National Archives has it, "The past is prologue to the future."

Suggested Essay Topics

1. Why does Nick compare the Dutch sailors to Gatsby? How does the comparison help to state Fitzgerald's conclusion?

2. How is the story an ironic twist of the American Dream? Consider Daisy and Gatsby, Daisy and Tom, Myrtle and George Wilson, Myrtle and Tom, Nick and Jordan.

3. Nick speaks of the "corruption" of Gatsby's guests and Gatsby's "incorruptible dream." How do these phrases begin to pull all the threads of the story together?

4. How does Fitzgerald make statements about pseudo-intellectualism?

5. Fitzgerald demonstrates the power of proper names. Prove this statement.

6. Compare the beginning and the ending of the novel. Has Gatsby changed? Has Nick changed? Explain and justify your responses.

Sample Analytical Paper Topics

The following paper topics are based on the entire book. Following each topic is a thesis and sample outline. Use these as a starting point for your paper.

Topic #1

Henry Steele Commager in *The American Mind: An Interpretation of American Thought and Character Since the 1880s* contends that "the tragedy is not that Gatsby lies dead, the rooms in his fabulous mansion silent—but that while he lived he realized all his ambitions." Justify this contention.

Outline

I.   Thesis Statement: *Although Gatsby's end was tragic, he was able to realize his ambitions.*

II. He fulfilled the ambition of acquiring money.

   A.   By illegal means, he acquired massive amounts of money.

III. He fulfilled the ambition of experiencing love.

   A.   By determination, he experienced a physical relationship with Daisy.

IV. He fulfilled the ambition of gaining popularity.

    A. Through generosity, he entertained hundreds of guests.

Topic #2

How do literary devices add to the dimension of depth or texture to this novel?

Outline

I. Thesis Statement: *Fitzgerald employs several devices, including color imagery, symbols, and descriptive tags, throughout the novel.*

II. Color imagery conveys dual meanings.

    A. Yellow is associated not only with bright, heavenly scenes, opulence, and wealth, but also with corruption and decay.

III. Symbols add meaning.

    A. Cars symbolize restlessness, driving ambition, recklessness.

    B. Eyes symbolize the presence or absence of God.

IV. Recurring "tags" of description characterize effectively.

    A. Jordan's "jauntiness" establishes her as atypical and yet representative of young women in the 1920s.

Topic #3

Prove that Gatsby really is worth more than "the whole damn bunch put together."

Outline

I. Thesis Statement: *Nick's assertion that Gatsby is worth more than "the whole damn bunch put together" is supported by Gatsby's purer motives and actions.*

II. Gatsby retains the American Dream in its purest form.

    A. He has the quality of the original seekers of the dream—the pursuit of life, liberty, and happiness.

III. He adheres to the precept of accepting consequences.

    A. Having "taken" Daisy that night in Louisville, he feels it is his responsibility to marry her.

IV. Gatsby possesses indefatigable hope.

    A. He believes Daisy will do the right thing, will make the moral choice she failed to make five years before, especially now that he can provide for her needs materially.

Topic #4

Show how literary techniques most effectively convey Fitzgerald's theme of waste in the American Dream.

Outline

I. Thesis Statement: *A primary theme of the novel is waste, which Fitzgerald conveys through not only the narrative, but with literary devices as well.*

II. Symbols effectively convey wasted energy.

    A. Cars, the green light, and the billboard of Dr. T. J. Eckleburg's eyes convey waste on different levels.

III. Imagery effectively conveys wasted lives.

    A. Color and heat images convey decadence.

IV. Naming effectively conveys wasted opportunity.

    A. Name of the novel, names of characters, and names of places suggest a waste of ideals.

V. Other devices convey the same theme.

    A. Settings

    B. Contrasts

Appendix
Timeline of *The Great Gatsby*

Since this novel is told as a series of flashbacks within a frame narrative, it is difficult to place events in their correct time order. The following timeline shows the actual chronology of events in the novel.

Age 17	Gatsby meets Dan Cody and learns about the leisure class.
October 1917	Gatsby meets Daisy. She is 18; Jordan is 16.
1918	She almost marries him.
1918	By fall "she is gay again."
June 1919	Daisy marries Tom Buchanan after receiving a $350,000 necklace. Gatsby is at Oxford.
August 1919	Tom is already having an affair.
April 1920	Daisy and Tom's daughter Pammy is born.
Autumn 1921	Nick comes back from the war.
Spring 1922	Nick comes to the East and sets up residence in West Egg, Long Island.
Summer 1922	The main action of the novel takes place.
Autumn 1922	Nick returns to the Midwest.

SECTION FIVE

Bibliography

Allen, Frederick Lewis. *Only Yesterday: An Informal History of the Nineteen-Twenties.* New York: Harper & Row, 1957.

Commager, Henry Steele. *The American Mind: An Interpretation of American Thought and Character Since the 1880s.* New Haven: Yale University Press, 1950.

Fitzgerald, F. Scott. *The Great Gatsby.* Preface and notes by Matthew J. Bruccoli. New York: Macmillan Publishing Company, 1992.

Holman, C. Hugh and Harmon, William. *Handbook to Literature.* New York: Macmillan Publishing Company, 1992.

Turnbull, Andrew. *Scott Fitzgerald.* New York: Charles Scribner's Sons, 1962.

Turnbull, Andrew, editor. *The* Letters of F. Scott Fitzgerald. New York: Charles Scribner's Sons, 1963.

NOTES

NOTES

NOTES

NOTES